To my parents, John and Janet, who have always encouraged me to pursue whatever crazy adventure I could think of - F.B.

BLOOMSBURY CHILDREN'S BOOKS
Bloomsbury Publishing Plc
50 Bedford Square, London, WC1B 3DP, UK

BLOOMSBURY, BLOOMSBURY CHILDREN'S BOOKS and the Diana logo are trademarks of Bloomsbury Publishing Plc

First published in Great Britain 2019 by Bloomsbury Publishing Plc

A catalogue record for this book is available from the British Library

ISBN: 978-1-5266-0112-4

2 4 6 8 10 9 7 5 3 1

Printed and bound in India by Replika Press Pvt. Ltd.

EPIC TALES OF TRIUMPH AND ADVENTURE

SIMON CHESHIRE
FATTI BURKE

BLOOMSBURY
CHILDREN'S BOOKS
LONDON OXFORD NEW YORK NEW DELHI SYDNEY

CONTENTS

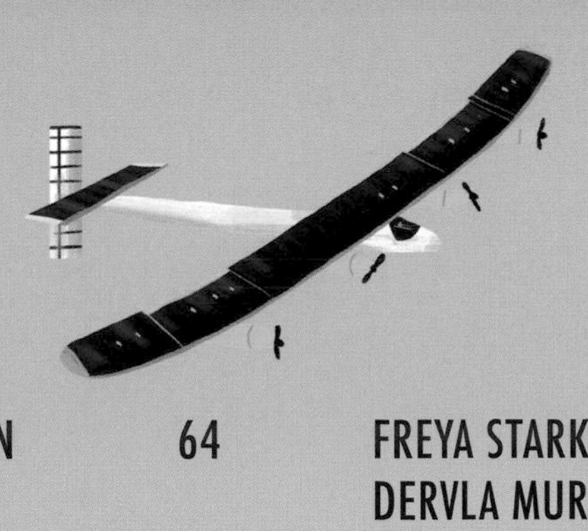

INTRODUCTION

If there's one thing human beings have always been fascinated with, it's an epic quest full of terrifying hurdles that must be overcome to reach a seemingly impossible goal. History is rich with real-life examples of extraordinary people who faced triumphs, perils and challenges that would make the rest of us hide under the kitchen table.

Most of these adventures were undertaken by choice, while others were the result of chance, necessity or immense courage in the face of danger. Many of the people you'll read about here are true heroes. Others did bad things as well as good things. A few of them are total villains, but they all made their mark on history.

NR-7952

YURI GAGARIN

COSMONAUT

At just after 6.00 a.m. on 12th April 1961, a voice crackled over a radio link: 'Preliminary stage ... intermediate ... main ... lift-off! We wish you a good flight. Everything is all right.' Imagine you're strapped into a padded seat, inside a metal sphere. Packed tightly around you are controls and instruments. You can't see out of the capsule, except for a tiny porthole close to your knees. That's where twenty-seven-year-old Russian cosmonaut Yuri Gagarin found himself that morning. He replied to the radio transmission, 'Let's go!'

YURI GAGARIN
1934–1968

Gagarin was one of twenty pilots chosen for the top secret Vostok programme, a vital part of the USSR's Space Race with the USA. The USSR, or Soviet Union, was a group of countries – led by Russia – that existed for most of the twentieth century. At first, none of the twenty pilots were told that the aim of this programme was to send a human being into space for the first time! Each pilot went through gruelling physical and mental tests to prepare them, such as being spun around at high speeds and solving complicated maths problems.

VOSTOK 1

The huge rocket that would eventually blast Gagarin and his *Vostok 1* capsule into space was a great technical achievement but a very risky one. The capsule had no back-up retrorockets for when it came time to return home, so enough food and water for ten days was put on board in case Gagarin had to wait for the capsule simply to drop out of the sky. The letters 'CCCP' (Russian for 'USSR') were painted onto Gagarin's helmet, just in case he landed in a foreign country and people wondered who he was.

Before the launch, Gagarin was understandably nervous. He was about to go on a very dangerous journey that would be a turning point for him, his country, the whole world and human history!

ORBITING EARTH

The *Vostok 1* mission, from start to finish, lasted just 108 minutes. To get into orbit, the rocket had to reach a speed of around 8 kilometres per second (29,000 kph). Once in space, the capsule spent just under an hour and a half doing one complete trip around the Earth, at an altitude of around 320 kilometres (200 miles).

Luckily, *Vostok's* one and only retrorocket fired correctly. The service module containing the last of the fuel was jettisoned, leaving the metal sphere Gagarin was strapped into as the re-entry module. It was shaped like a ball partly to make it more aerodynamic and partly so that, as it tumbled back to Earth, everything inside – including Gagarin – could swivel and stay upright.

Yuri Gargarin gazes in wonder at Earth below.

BACK ON SOLID GROUND

With no other rockets to slow the capsule's fall and only a parachute to reduce its speed, it would hit the ground too fast for its pilot to survive. At a height of 7 kilometres (4 miles), seconds before impact, Gagarin had to open the large hatch above his head and float down to the ground on a parachute of his own. He landed in a field 2,800 kilometres (1,730 miles) west of where he'd been aiming for, but at least he was alive!

Within days, he would become the most famous man on the planet. The Soviet government treated their hero like gold and wouldn't let him go into space again in case he wasn't so lucky next time.

Many years later, after he died, the little village where he was born was renamed Gagarin in his honour. To this day, cosmonauts being taken by bus to the launch pad mark his achievement by doing the same last-minute thing that he did – they stop the bus and go for a wee!

ALOHA WANDERWELL

WORLD EXPLORER

In the autumn of 1922, an advertisement appeared in the *Paris Herald: 'Brains, Beauty & Breeches – World Tour Offer for Lucky Young Woman'.*

Idris Hall, a rebellious sixteen-year-old from Canada, spotted it and knew instantly that she was going to be that 'Lucky Young Woman'. She had grown up dreaming about exciting adventures and this ad was completely irresistible to her.

The ad had been placed by a Polish man called Valerian Johannes Pieczynski, also known as 'Captain' Walter Wanderwell (who would later encourage Idris to call herself Aloha Wanderwell). He was a controversial character who'd been imprisoned during World War I on suspicion of working for the Germans.

THE MILLION DOLLAR WAGER

Aloha met him and quickly secured her place on the Wanderwell Expedition, which was attracting a lot of public interest and was billed in the papers as 'The Million Dollar Wager'. The expedition was a race around the world in two Ford Model T cars to see which team could visit the most countries - one car was driven by Walter and the other by his wife, Nell. Aloha spoke several languages and was hired as a translator and secretary. However, she soon found herself behind the wheel of Walter's car, *Little Lizzie,* and behind the lens of a movie camera that was recording the entire trip! Nell and the whole idea of a race between husband and wife were soon ignored.

The Wanderwells were the 1920s equivalent of travel bloggers. Film, photos and first-hand accounts of their adventures kept the world informed about their progress. Aloha, with her self-confidence and striking looks, was the star of the show and became an international sensation. She and Walter, wearing their trademark riding breeches, leather flying helmets and military-style jackets, were pictured in one exotic location after another.

THE MOST TRAVELLED

Despite the glamorous sheen, Walter and Aloha faced regular dangers and setbacks, from civil wars to rickety rope bridges. They ended up using crushed bananas as a substitute for engine grease and water mixed with elephant fat instead of oil. In India and Africa, oxen were needed to tow the car across mudflats and rivers. In China, when they couldn't get any fuel, farm labourers pulled the Model T like carthorses for 130 kilometres (80 miles).

By the time the expedition ended in 1925, Aloha was nineteen, had travelled through forty-three countries on four continents and was dubbed 'The Most Travelled Girl in the World'. But it didn't end there! Aloha kept travelling and making films for most of her life. She married Walter and they had two children together. Aloha Wanderwell was an extraordinary person, who today is considered a pioneer of feminism and an important figure in early documentary film-making.

Aloha and Captain Wanderwell travel through the jungle with *Little Lizzie*.

CAPTAIN JAMES COOK

EXPLORER AND NAVIGATOR

James Cook, son of a humble farm worker from Yorkshire, England, was perhaps the greatest explorer of the eighteenth century. He made three voyages around the Pacific Ocean in his ambition to go, as he wrote, 'farther than any man has been before me ... as far as I think it possible for man to go.'

CAPTAIN JAMES COOK
1728–1779

THE FIRST VOYAGE (1768–1771)

Lieutenant Cook, as he was then, set sail aboard the British Royal Navy ship *Endeavour*, accompanied by a selection of scientists who would collect all kinds of previously unknown specimens along the way. Part of their mission was to observe the planet Venus from the southern hemisphere in order to help astronomers back home learn more about this fascinating planet.

Once Cook and his shipmates had completed their observations, they went off in search of the mythical Great Southern Continent, *Terra Australis*. This vast land mass was rumoured to occupy the bottom of the world, and had been appearing on maps as complete guesswork since the 1500s.

In his quest to find this mythical continent, Cook sailed around New Zealand, mapping it with pinpoint accuracy. He then journeyed up the unexplored eastern coast of Australia (at that time called New Holland), landing at Botany Bay, near modern Sydney. HMS *Endeavour* nearly sank when it hit the Great Barrier Reef, and while making repairs, over thirty of the crew died of malaria, fevers and dysentery.

Eventually Cook and the rest of the crew had to give up in their hunt for the lost land mass and they returned to England.

THE SECOND VOYAGE (1772–1775)

Annoyed that he never found that missing continent, Cook set out once more in two ships – the *Adventure* and the *Resolution*. He would either find *Terra Australis* or prove once and for all that it didn't exist. The ships sailed close to the shores of Antarctica but were forced back by the cold, and changed their route to journey via New Zealand and Tahiti. Here they came across Easter Island, the Marquesas, Tonga and the New Hebrides. Cook didn't discover them – all these places were already home to indigenous people. However, as far as Europeans were concerned, Cook turned these islands from vague reports and places seen from afar into scientific facts. His first two voyages had essentially mapped out the South Pacific.

THE THIRD VOYAGE (1776–1780)

In 1776, Cook set out once more aboard *Resolution,* this time accompanied by the ship *Discovery*. He was on the hunt for another myth! The North-West Passage was a fabled route through the Americas, linking the Pacific to the Atlantic. He didn't find it, but he did come across the Hawaiian Islands. At first, he and his crew got on so well with the islanders that they assumed he was some sort of god! However, a squabble over a stolen boat got out of hand and Cook was murdered. A monument now stands on the spot where he fell.

Despite having a quick temper, Captain Cook treated his crews well and was considered a good leader. He also accidentally helped rid the high seas of scurvy: he had no idea that poor nutrition caused the disease, but he did know that nutrient-rich pickled cabbage kept it at bay. So he took several tons of it on his voyages!

Captain Cook sets his sights on new discoveries in far-off lands.

ZENOBIA

QUEEN

Said to be highly intelligent and well educated, with eyes as dark as midnight and teeth so white they looked like pearls, Zenobia came from the province of Palmyra (Syria today), part of the Roman Empire.

Zenobia married Odaenathus, governor of Palmyra. At this time, the Roman Empire was far from secure. It was frequently attacked by tribes from the north and was plagued by political squabbles – in the previous fifty years it had twenty-six different emperors! The province of Palmyra had always had good relations with Rome, especially after Odaenathus helped send some Persian packing. Odaenathus took advantage of this favour by taking charge of all Rome's territory in the Middle East and calling himself its king.

When Odaenathus was killed in 267 CE, Zenobia took over and called herself queen. Technically, she ruled on behalf of her young son, Vaballathus, but she was very much in charge. She encouraged learning, diversity and religious freedom, but was also every bit as ambitious as her husband. With so much fighting over the throne in Rome, it wasn't too far-fetched to think that a strong leader from the eastern provinces could become emperor – if not Zenobia, then perhaps her son.

As a child, she'd become an expert at horse riding. It was a useful skill when she began leading her army across borders and conquering territory. By 271 CE, she'd done so much conquering that she ruled a massive area covering parts of modern Iraq and Syria, west across Turkey and south to Egypt. It was a Palmyran empire that might one day rival Rome's!

THE BATTLE OF IMMAE

Meanwhile, Rome's latest emperor was the military commander Aurelian. He most certainly wasn't going to stand for Zenobia's empire-building and marched against her. Meeting on a wide, flat plain, the Romans goaded the Palmyrans into launching an all-out charge. The Romans turned and ran, appearing to flee. They let the enemy chase them until the Palmyrans became completely exhausted (their heavy battle gear wore them out quickly). Once the Palmyrans were tired, the Romans turned and charged – and inflicted a serious defeat!

Zenobia and Vaballathus were captured soon after.

ZENOBIA'S LEGEND

Historical records of Zenobia's birth, life, reign and death are all at odds with each other. One thing nobody can agree on is what happened to her in the end. She might have lived peacefully in exile in Italy for the rest of her days, she might have been dragged through the streets of Rome in chains and executed, she might have died of disease on the way to Rome or she might even have killed herself rather than face Aurelian's revenge. What can be agreed is that she was one of the most powerful women in the history of the Roman Empire.

Oddly enough, despite her great influence, no statue or great picture of Zenobia has ever been found that dates back to when she was alive. We only have a few small pictures on coins from the time of her reign.

Zenobia charges against the Roman Empire.

ROBIN KNOX-JOHNSTON ELLEN MACARTHUR LAURA DEKKER

SAILORS

There aren't many sporting challenges that are as physically and mentally challenging as sailing around the world on your own. Imagine sitting completely alone, in a sailing boat, surrounded by thousands of kilometres of rolling ocean. All that can get you home is the force of the wind and your own skill at navigating. It's a trip that takes enormous courage and true determination.

ROBIN KNOX-JOHNSTON

In 1968, *The Sunday Times* newspaper announced a new sailing race around the world. The Golden Globe had to be completed solo, without stopping – something which had never been done before. An experienced sailor, Robin Knox-Johnston was one of nine entrants, and in June 1968 he left Falmouth in Cornwall, UK, on his 9.8-metre-long boat, *Suhaili,* for a journey like no other.

By the time Knox-Johnston approached the Cape of Good Hope, on the southern tip of Africa, he was in second place. On his journey there he had already experienced problems: the boat started leaking and he had to make underwater repairs, the fresh water tanks had become contaminated with seawater and the boat's two-way radio had broken.

Without the radio, there was no way to communicate and he had no contact with the outside world for the next eight months. Having no radio caused navigation problems too, because he couldn't get accurate time checks to calculate his position, and having no weather forecasts meant no warning of storms or high seas ahead. But Knox-Johnston persevered, despite so many obstacles.

Of the nine starters, four dropped out before even getting past the Atlantic Ocean, one got as far as South Africa, one sank, one cheated and one got fed up and sailed to Tahiti! Only Knox-Johnston finished the race, in 312 days, and won the £5,000 prize.

Knox-Johnston
encounters a leak
on his round-the-
world trip.

ELLEN MacARTHUR

From a very young age, Ellen MacArthur was a dedicated sailor. For years she saved every penny she had so she could buy boating equipment. She even moved her bed into her parents' garage to make room for all her sailing equipment!

ELLEN MACARTHUR
b. 1976

HER FIRST ATTEMPT

The first of her two non-stop solo voyages was the 2001 Vendée Globe, a race run every four years and considered the world's greatest test in ocean sailing. MacArthur's custom-built 18-metre yacht, *Kingfisher,* contained a cabin about the size of a small car, packed with everything she'd need, including freeze-dried food and a tiny gas cooker. Having nobody else on board meant she had to train herself to sleep for just twenty or forty minutes at a time with a special once-a-week treat of a two-hour snooze.

In colder waters, big icebergs became a regular danger, and on one occasion she woke from a nap to find herself just a few metres from one. Even small chunks of ice (called 'growlers') could cause severe damage to the boat's hull. Sails became torn and at one point, in high winds, the boat tipped over on to its side.

Despite setbacks, her skill kept her in the race. Towards the finish, she was in with a chance of taking the lead but *Kingfisher* struck an object in the water, probably a half-submerged container that had fallen off a ship, and part of the steering system was damaged. MacArthur lost a day hauling the broken piece (which weighed more than she did!) back on board, and by then a win was out of her grasp. She came in second, with a time of just over 94 days.

Ellen MacArthur on her trimaran contesting with dangerous icebergs.

SETTING SAIL AGAIN

Four years later, she set out again. This time, she wasn't competing in an organised race but making an attempt to break the solo, non-stop record of 72 days, 22 hours and 54 minutes, held by Francis Joyon of France.

On this second voyage, the weather was worse. As well as icebergs, MacArthur had to deal with violent hailstorms and waves so huge that her trimaran (a boat with three hulls) teetered at the top of them as if on the edge of a cliff above a deep valley. One storm lasted three days and nights, with the boat in constant danger of overturning – during that period she managed a total of twenty minutes' sleep. Twice she had to climb up the 30-metre mast to make repairs while being swung around by the wind, which she described as being like trying to hang on to a wet telegraph pole in an earthquake.

But MacArthur didn't give up and finally reached home in a triumphant 71 days, 14 hours and 18 minutes, breaking the record. She was only twenty-eight at the time of her second trip around the world, but some have made similar voyages while still at school ...

LAURA DEKKER

Laura Dekker from the Netherlands was only fourteen when she announced in a Dutch newspaper that she intended to make a two-year trip around the world alone (not non-stop – the plan was for various breaks along the way). She was an expert sailor and had spent most of her early years at sea, sailing with her parents.

A ROUND-THE-WORLD TRIP

Many, including the Dutch authorities, were alarmed that someone so young wanted to attempt something so dangerous. It wasn't until August 2010 that Dekker finally set off from Gibraltar in her 11.5-metre yacht, *Guppy* (every boat she'd ever owned had been called *Guppy*), heading across the Atlantic, through the Panama Canal, over the north coast of Australia and around the Cape of Good Hope.

She completed the trip in 518 days, including stops. At 16 years and 123 days old, Dekker was the youngest person to sail solo around the world.

Laura Dekker on board Guppy *as she becomes the youngest person to sail around the world alone.*

LOUIS BLÉRIOT

AVIATOR

Just before Christmas 1903, American brothers Orville and Wilbur Wright made the world's first powered flight. It lasted one minute. That event kicked off an international scramble to design aircraft of all kinds – flying was the latest technological marvel!

Within a few years, Louis Blériot was France's leading aviator. He was a skilled engineer who'd made money inventing lamps for another recent invention, the automobile, and he put every penny he had into making and testing flying machines, starting with gliders he called the *Blériot I* and *Blériot II*. By the time he got to the *Blériot XI*, he had a lightweight, propeller-driven monoplane (one with a single set of wings, unlike most early aircraft, which had two sets, one above the other). It featured the three-fin tail design that's still used today and was powered by a 25-horsepower engine (by comparison, jet engines for modern planes can output up to 110,000 horsepower). Its wingspan was 7 metres and it was made mostly of nothing more than wood, wire and fabric.

BLÉRIOT TAKES TO THE SKIES

Blériot wanted to be the first person to cross the English Channel – an adventure that could win him £1,000 (which would be well over £100,000 in today's money). However, there was one issue – the *Blériot XI* had never flown for more than twenty minutes. Crossing the Channel, a distance of 37.8 kilometres (23.5 miles), would take *twice* that time! Undeterred, Blériot took off from Calais, France, as dawn broke on 25th July 1909.

This was not going to be an easy trip. Blériot was in a lot of pain from an injured foot, which had been badly burnt during a test flight. Now that he'd taken off, the weather was getting steadily murkier. The fragile monoplane kept to a height of around 75 metres. Travelling at about 65 kph (40 mph), it was soon ahead of the small ship that was acting as its escort across the Channel. Blériot had no compass and no flight instruments on board, so once he lost sight of the escort ship the dull skies meant he couldn't see either the French or English coasts. He had no way of knowing his exact position and kept on course by sight and instinct alone.

Louis Blériot takes off over the English Channel.

WHEELS DOWN IN DOVER

Blériot pushed on, determined to reach his goal as rain poured down and the winds around him began to howl, making visibility even worse. By the time he spotted the white cliffs of Dover, the wind had picked up and was causing serious problems. Swerving around several buildings, he made a heavy landing in a field near Dover Castle, watched by a small crowd of onlookers. The monoplane's undercarriage and propeller were smashed up, but he'd made it! Louis Blériot won the £1,000 prize and made headlines all over the world.

The original *Blériot XI* never flew again, although it was repaired and put on show at Selfridges department store in London. Blériot turned his fame as a daring aviator into a successful aircraft-making business. His factory turned out hundreds of *XIs*, with various modifications, and by 1910 his flying machines had set records for flight duration, altitude, speed and distance.

MARY KINGSLEY

WRITER AND EXPLORER

For the first thirty years of her life, Mary Kingsley did what most women in Victorian England did: stayed at home. She spent her time tucked away in her father's library, reading true-life accounts of adventure and exploration. When both her parents died in 1892, Mary inherited enough money to pursue her travel ambitions.

MARY KINGSLEY
1862–1900

EXPLORING AFRICA

At the time, West Africa was considered a place of deadly danger for even the toughest, most experienced traveller. It was certainly no place for a woman who'd barely left her own home. Naturally, she paid no attention to this view and set out on her adventures. She made two major trips into western and equatorial Africa, exploring areas around Sierra Leone, Angola, Gabon and what is now Nigeria. She lived with local tribespeople, learning about their societies, their religions and their way of life. However, one English custom she never let go was the Victorian ladies' dress code, which she upheld at all times (and which must have been extremely uncomfortable in the hot African climate!).

She also faced a terrifying array of dangers. She hacked through dense rainforest, waded through mangrove swamps, travelled down rapids and along crocodile-infested river systems, all the while being on her guard against a variety of poisonous creatures, including snakes and scorpions.

Perhaps her scariest moment came while navigating the Ogooué River by canoe to meet the Fang tribe. They were cannibals and the only other European who'd seen them had mysteriously vanished. As Mary arrived with her small group of local tribesmen, the Fang raced out of their village, weapons held high, clearly intending to attack. Mary ordered her companions to stay still and hold out their hands in a gesture of friendship. At the last moment, the Fang recognised one of her group and death was narrowly averted!

Mary Kingsley hacks through dense forests on her adventures.

SOUVENIRS FROM HER TRAVELS

Throughout her travels, Mary carried a knife and a pistol for protection, but despite all of the danger she faced, she never used them. She preferred instead to rely on her wits and local knowledge. On behalf of the British Museum, she collected plant and animal specimens, returning with new species of insects, reptiles and fish.

Back home, she wrote about her experiences and gave lectures on African society. She also became a passionate critic of European interference in Africa, condemning Christian missionaries for damaging local religious and social beliefs.

In 1898, she volunteered to serve in the Boer War in South Africa as a nurse. It's perhaps cruelly ironic that, having avoided numerous tropical diseases and infections on her travels, she died of a fever there. Bold and forthright to the last, she asked to be left to die alone, so that nobody would see her in a weakened condition.

THOR HEYERDAHL

ADVENTURER

Thor Heyerdahl uses the stars to navigate a path across the Pacific Ocean.

Thor Heyerdahl wanted to prove a theory: that Polynesia – the huge scattering of more than one thousand islands across the central and southern Pacific – was first inhabited by people who'd drifted there on rafts from South America. And he was willing to set out on some hair-raisingly dangerous sea voyages to prove his point ...

In 1946, Heyerdahl presented his ideas to a group of experts on the subject. Nonsense, they said, Polynesia was reached from the Far East, in the opposite direction. In ancient times, the technology simply didn't exist to make such a journey possible. But Heyerdahl firmly believed he was right and decided to set sail in order to gain the proof he needed.

THE *KON-TIKI*

Heyerdahl assembled a five-man crew of friends and they recreated exactly the sort of raft that would have been built at the time, using only ancient techniques and materials. It was around 9 metres long and 4.5 metres wide, built by tying nine big balsa wood logs together with hemp ropes. A bamboo cabin with a roof made from banana leaves was all they had for shelter. The only way to steer the raft was by its sail or using paddles. Heyerdahl called it the *Kon-Tiki*, after the ancient Inca god of the sun, and the bearded face of the god was painted on to the sail.

In April 1947, they set out from the coast of Peru, the raft creaking as it bobbed on the water. Although they had a modern radio with them for communication, and carried most of their drinking water in cans, they stuck as far as possible to the kind of supplies the Incas would have had, including sweet potatoes, coconuts and other fruit, plus fish caught along the way. The plan was to drift, using the prevailing Pacific water currents to carry the *Kon-Tiki* along. Navigation would be by sun, stars and winds, just like in ancient times.

Almost nobody expected Heyerdahl and his crew to survive.

LAND AHOY!

The small raft faced rough seas, with waves often taller than the mast, and the crew saw a variety of marine life, including powerful sharks and enormous whales. On the ninety-third day of their voyage, they finally glimpsed land on the horizon. Just over a week later, at daybreak, a reef was spotted close by. The *Kon-Tiki* was badly damaged by the jagged coral but the crew made it to land safely, to find that they had achieved their goal: they were at the Raroia coral atoll in the Tuamotu group of islands. They were rescued by a French schooner, which took them to nearby Tahiti along with the battered *Kon-Tiki*.

Heyerdahl wrote a book about the whole adventure, which became a big hit all over the world. He went on to make a number of other, equally daring voyages, notably the *Ra* and *Ra II* expeditions, in which he sailed an ancient Egyptian reed boat across the Atlantic Ocean.

Although *Kon-Tiki* had proved that making such a journey was possible, despite what the experts said, Heyerdahl's theory about the origins of the Polynesian people remained controversial. To this day, his ideas are widely disputed.

NANCY WAKE
NOOR INAYAT KHAN
KRYSTYNA SKARBEK

SOE AGENTS

During World War II, large areas of mainland Europe were taken over by the Nazis. The Special Operations Executive was a top-secret organisation set up to help Britain and its allies in these occupied areas by using undercover agents. To be an SOE agent, what you needed more than anything else was sheer nerve. Female agents were among the SOE's best because, in those days, soldiers and spies were generally assumed to be men! This meant that a woman could, for example, carry secret papers in a shopping basket and go unnoticed, while a man carrying the same papers in a package might look suspicious.

NANCY WAKE – 'THE WHITE MOUSE'

By the time the high-spirited, no-nonsense New Zealander Nancy Wake joined the SOE in 1944, she'd already saved hundreds of lives working for the underground French Resistance movement, smuggling soldiers and civilians out of the south of France. She was on the run from the Nazis, who called her 'the, White Mouse' because she kept evading capture.

As an SOE agent, she co-ordinated small groups of fighters totalling over 7,000 people. She was so good at organising and hiding her network that a force of over 20,000 German troops couldn't stop their activities.

Nancy Wake cycles for three days and nights with urgent news.

An important aspect of Nancy Wake's mission in France was keeping communications going between London and the Resistance. On one occasion, when codes for radio messages were lost, she got word to the Allies by cycling for three days and nights, travelling 500 kilometres (310 miles) to reach another radio and then return before her absence raised suspicions.

NOOR INAYAT KHAN – CODE NAME 'MADELEINE'

Noor Inayat Khan lived in London but had been born in Russia, the daughter of an Indian prince. She was reserved and a little awkward, the last person you would expect to be a spy. She was also a published writer of poetry and children's stories and was deeply influenced by pacifism (the belief that violence is never justified).

Nevertheless, she volunteered for military service in 1940 and became a skilled wireless telegraph operator. Her steely determination to help the war effort got her assigned to the SOE. Disguised as a nurse called Jeanne-Marie Regnier and using the code name 'Madeleine', she went to Paris in 1943 and began work with the French Resistance, passing vital information to and from Britain.

UNDERCOVER IN PARIS

Less than a week after she arrived, her group was discovered by the Nazis. Agents and Resistance fighters were swiftly rounded up, one after another. But Khan managed to avoid being caught and was soon the only agent left!

Her SOE trainers had seriously doubted that anyone as sensitive as her could be suitable for undercover work. If the worst happened, they thought, she'd crumple like a wet tissue.

Khan proved them *very* wrong! London told her to run. She refused. She was the only radio link to the UK left in Paris and she would not abandon her post. Any agents still in the city or the surrounding areas needed her more than ever and, for three months, Noor Khan continued to evade capture. Almost every day, with her radio equipment in tow, she moved to a new location and switched disguises. With astonishing bravery, she continued to relay messages for the Resistance.

Noor Inayat Khan travels through the streets of Paris in disguise.

Even when she was finally captured, betrayed by a double agent, she kept her cool. At first, she fed false information to the Nazis but after two escape attempts – both of which nearly succeeded – she became the first British agent sent to the high-security Pforzheim prison in Germany. In September 1944, she was executed. Witnesses said that with her last breath she uttered the French word *liberté*, meaning 'freedom'.

KRYSTYNA SKARBEK – CODE NAME 'CHRISTINE GRANVILLE'

Krystyna Skarbek was from Poland, a royal countess who arrived in London shortly after the start of the war. She was outgoing and self-confident, quick thinking, cool under pressure and seemed almost to enjoy being in dangerous situations! Winston Churchill once called her 'my favourite spy'.

She completed many missions disguised as a news reporter. Several times she parachuted into Hungary, skied over the Carpathian Mountains into Poland, made contact with the Resistance and skied out again! Skarbek made so much trouble for the Nazis in Poland that posters were put up in every railway station offering a large reward for her capture.

Krystyna Skarbek whistles outside a prison, passing secret code to someone inside.

On an early mission in Poland, her real name was suddenly called out loudly in a coffee shop full of Nazis. She'd been spotted by an old friend who had no idea she was a spy. Skarbek calmly persuaded her friend that she was mistaken then sat and drank her coffee until the Nazis were no longer suspicious.

A RESCUE MISSION

Her most daring mission was the rescue of three other SOE agents in France in 1944. To check the agents were being held in a particular prison, she walked around outside it, whistling a tune until one of them whistled it back. She then went inside and told the guards that she was a British agent and that thousands of Allied troops were advancing nearby. She convinced the guards that if they hadn't let their prisoners go by the time the troops arrived, they'd be in serious trouble. She was so stern and confident that the guards fell for it and released the agents!

The fact that the SOE even existed was kept secret from all but a handful of people in the British government. After World War II, the identities and exploits of SOE agents, both male and female, remained largely unknown for many years. In 2009, a small monument to the organisation was put up on the south bank of the Thames in London, opposite the Houses of Parliament.

MATTHEW WEBB

SWIMMER

His name isn't well known today, but Matthew Webb was one of Britain's most celebrated heroes of the nineteenth century. Water was in Webb's blood! One of fourteen siblings, he taught himself to swim and, at the age of twelve, he joined the merchant navy as an apprentice and served on a variety of vessels. In 1875, Webb became the first person to swim the English Channel unaided.

MATTHEW WEBB
1848—1883

A NATIONAL HERO

His Channel swim wasn't his first brush with fame. In 1872, he was first mate on a Cunard Line passenger ship, the *Russia*. Halfway across the Atlantic, a man fell overboard. Without hesitating, Webb dived into the freezing waters and spent thirty-five minutes trying to find the missing passenger. Sadly he couldn't, but the story caught the attention of the British press, who made him a national hero, and his bravery won him an award. As if that wasn't enough, the following year he also saved his younger brother Thomas from drowning in the river back home.

AN IMPOSSIBLE AMBITION

As soon as he heard that someone had recently tried, and failed, to swim across the Channel – something considered all but impossible – Webb knew he'd found his life's ambition. He left his job and became a full-time swimmer. To reach his goal, he'd need to swim the narrowest section of the Channel, the Strait of Dover, from Dover, England, to Cap Griz-Nez at Calais, France, a distance of around 37.8 kilometres (just under 23 miles).

After much training, by the summer of 1875, Webb was ready. His first attempt, on 12th August, was a disaster when strong winds and choppy seas forced him to turn back. But Webb wasn't going to give up that easily and two weeks later he tried again.

WEBB SWIMS FOR GLORY

The weather was better this time and he dived into the sea with determination and focus, his body covered in porpoise fat to keep out the icy cold of the water. Flanked by three small support boats, he set off at a steady breaststroke. The crossing was a gruelling feat of endurance. After eight hours, already tired, he got a painful sting from a jellyfish. But Webb swam on. Tidal movements pulled him a long way off course; so much so that instead of 37 kilometres he swam nearly double that, a massive 64 kilometres. For five hours, strong currents off Calais prevented him from reaching France. But still Webb swam on. By the time he arrived, totally exhausted, he'd been in the water 21 hours, 45 minutes.

He'd done it! He was now an even bigger hero than ever. For the rest of his life, he gave lectures, swam in competitions and took part in special events and stunts, including floating in a tank of water for 128 hours! As a major celebrity, Webb endorsed products and appeared on merchandise – everything from commemorative mugs to boxes of matches.

Matthew Webb swims fearlessly across the Channel.

JAN MORRIS
JUNKO TABEI

MOUNTAINEERS

Mount Everest is an *extremely* hostile place: -40°C on average, with hurricane winds, fierce storms and air so thin near the summit it can cause severe damage to your body if you don't use oxygen tanks ... that's if an avalanche or a bone-breaking fall doesn't get you first! Why attempt such a dangerous climb? George Mallory's famous answer was 'because it's there'. His 1924 expedition was among the first to try for the top, but he and his team never returned.

Morris makes a daring dash down Everest.

The first people to reach the summit, 8,850 metres above sea level, were Edmund Hillary from New Zealand and Tenzing Norgay from Tibet, part of a large expedition in 1953. Arriving at the top of the world at 11.30 a.m. on 29th May, they spent fifteen minutes there, took photos and left some chocolates.

JAN MORRIS

Among the members of the 1953 expedition was a journalist from Wales. Morris had served in the army during World War II and was now a reporter for *The Times* newspaper in London. As soon as the climbers returned, Morris made a hair-raising dash down from Base Camp 6,700 metres up to reach a radio transmitter and deliver the momentous news. Darkness was closing in, the ice underfoot was crumbling and Morris, hurrying as fast as possible, could barely stay on two feet! The report – sent using a code to avoid leaks – made history and Morris went on to have a highly acclaimed career as a journalist, novelist, historian and travel writer.

Morris's own life story is historic too. At the time of the Everest expedition, his name was James Morris, but following surgery in 1972 her name became Jan. She had the immense courage to be publicly open and honest about her transition, at a time when gender identity was far less understood and discussed than it is today.

JUNKO TABEI

Since 1953, many people have made the challenging climb to the summit of Mount Everest. One of the most notable climbers is Junko Tabei, a multi-record-breaking mountaineer from Japan, who caught the climbing bug at the age of ten after a school trip to the volcanic Mount Nasu.

In the 1960s, Tabei set up Japan's Ladies Climbing Club and they formed a fifteen-woman group who planned to climb Everest in 1975. Shortly after midnight on 4th May, while they were 6,300 metres up the mountain, an avalanche suddenly buried them alive as they slept! Tabei was tangled up in her tent and began to suffocate. Fortunately, their Sherpa guides quickly rescued them and nobody was badly hurt. Undeterred, they continued climbing after a few days' recovery and on 16th May Tabei became the first woman to reach the summit.

Junko Tabei eventually climbed the highest peaks in over seventy countries. In 1992, she became the first woman to climb the tallest mountains on all seven continents, including Mount Kilimanjaro in Africa and Mount Vinson in Antarctica.

Junko Tabei is rescued from a sudden avalanche.

HOWARD CARTER

ARCHAEOLOGIST

In November 1922, a tall, rather quiet man with a faint Norfolk accent made the greatest archaeological discovery in history. Howard Carter had spent years organising digs all over the Valley of the Kings in Egypt, looking for ancient tombs. He'd found precisely nothing and the wealthy sponsor of his work, Lord Carnarvon, was running out of money and patience.

HOWARD CARTER
1874–1939

THE SEARCH CONTINUES

Carter remained convinced that the last resting place of a little-known pharaoh called Tutankhamun, who'd only reigned for a few years and died young, was out there somewhere. Finally, after years of searching, Carter found what he'd been looking for!

The discovery began when a flat surface was uncovered by Carter's team of Egyptian workers. They found an edge and realised it was a stone step, then quickly dug out more, leading down to a doorway sealed with plaster. Ancient hieroglyphs were just visible on its surface. Behind the seal was a corridor, filled with stone chippings. Once that was cleared, a second seal was revealed. The cartouches (names in hieroglyphs) on this were clearer: Tut-ankh-amun ... Tut-ankh-amun ... Tut-ankh-amun ...

Carter's growing excitement was dampened by only one thing: the top left corners of both seals had obviously been broken and re-sealed thousands of years ago. Someone *had* been into the tomb. It was likely that the burial chambers were empty, just like every other discovery in the Valley.

THE TOMB OPENS

Carter had already sent word to Carnarvon, who hurried to Egypt along with his daughter, Lady Evelyn Herbert. On the afternoon of 26th November, they stood in front of the second seal as Carter cut a small hole through it with a hammer and chisel, caking the sweltering corridor with dust.

As the seal was breached, a hot flow of air emerged, as if the tomb was letting go its dying gasp. Carter made the hole large enough to put his arm through. He held the candle out as far as he could, peering into the darkness beyond.

'What can you see?' called Carnarvon.

Howard Carter discovers amazing treasures in an ancient tomb.

'Wonderful things,' said Carter.

The chamber was heaped with ancient treasures. The flickering light from Carter's candle reflected off the shining glow of gold.

AN ANCIENT MASK

That night Carter secretly returned, along with Carnarvon and Lady Evelyn. He knew that word of their discovery would spread like lightning and that he had to assess the tomb properly before the media circus started.

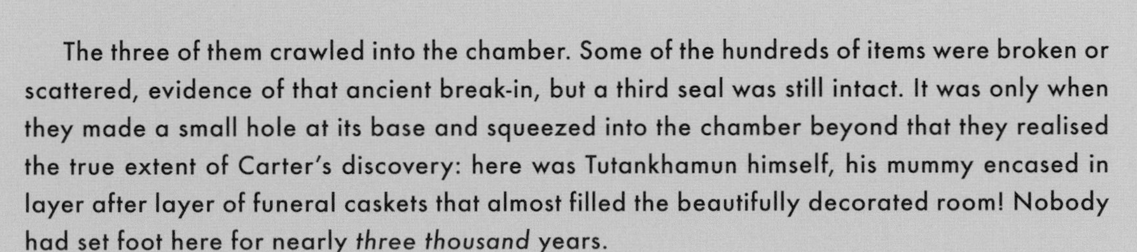

The three of them crawled into the chamber. Some of the hundreds of items were broken or scattered, evidence of that ancient break-in, but a third seal was still intact. It was only when they made a small hole at its base and squeezed into the chamber beyond that they realised the true extent of Carter's discovery: here was Tutankhamun himself, his mummy encased in layer after layer of funeral caskets that almost filled the beautifully decorated room! Nobody had set foot here for nearly *three thousand* years.

It was the most complete ancient tomb ever found and took ten years to empty and catalogue. Today, its contents are preserved in Cairo, the capital of Egypt. Many of its treasures are on display, including what is now one of the most famous objects in the world – Tutankhamun's funeral mask.

ANNE BONNY
MARY READ

PIRATES

The years 1650 to 1720 are sometimes called the Golden Age of Piracy, a period associated with buried treasure, eye patches, parrots on shoulders, raise the Jolly Roger, me hearties, yo-ho-ho. However, hardly any of that stuff is true! Another myth is that all pirates were men ...

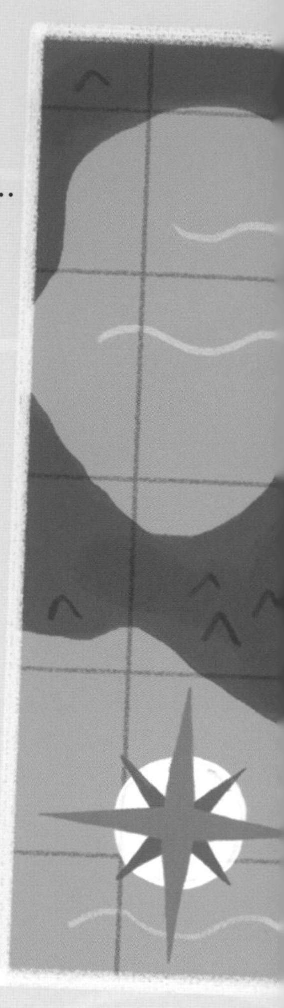

Anne Bonny and Mary Read were notorious pirates who travelled on the same ship under the command of 'Calico' Jack Rackham and gained a reputation for fearless fighting and fiery tempers. Both had been raised as boys – in each case as part of a parental scam to get allowance money out of a relative!

ANNE BONNY

Bonny, originally from Ireland, met Jack Rackham in the Bahamas. He wasn't exactly the most successful pirate around. He was known more for his colourful clothes than his pirating, but his fortunes improved once Anne Bonny joined the crew.

Legend has it that she once captured a French merchant ship single-handed. She made a fake dead body and covered it with red paint. As the ship approached, they could see her holding up the dummy with an axe raised above her head, yelling blood-curdling cries! The ship's crew were so terrified that they gave in without a fight.

MARY READ

Mary Read joined Bonny and Rackham after they raided the ship she was travelling on. She and Bonny became close friends and Read was soon every bit as fearsome and cut-throat as her crewmates. This was partly because she'd spent several years – disguised as a man – fighting with the English and Dutch armed forces.

Rackham's crew attacked ships all around Jamaica and the West Indies. Bonny and Read were always in the thick of it, handkerchiefs tied around their heads to soak up sweat, a sword in one hand and a pistol in the other.

THE END OF THE CREW

However, their luck didn't last. In October 1720, a sloop (a sailing ship with a single mast) crept up on Rackham's ship late at night. It was a 'King's ship' hired by the governor of Jamaica to hunt down pirates.

Anne Bonny and Mary Read rule the seas aboard their pirate ship.

The captain called on Rackham and his crew to surrender. Bonny and Read were the only ones who stood their ground. Rackham fled into the ship's cargo hold, where the rest of the pirates were hiding, all of them too terrified to face the governor's men. Alone, Bonny and Read fought back for as long as they could. At one point, Read yelled down into the hold, 'If there's a man among you, come up and fight!' to no avail.

Rackham, Bonny, Read and the rest of the pirate crew were put on trial in Jamaica and sentenced to death. Bonny and Read, under what was known as 'pleading the belly', both said they were pregnant and so couldn't be executed according to English law.

Mary Read died of fever in prison the following year. What became of Anne Bonny, nobody knows.

NEIL ARMSTRONG
EDWIN 'BUZZ' ALDRIN
MICHAEL COLLINS

ASTRONAUTS

For forty years after World War II, there was an intense rivalry between Russia and the USA, known as the Cold War. An important part of that rivalry was the Space Race. Russia, then known as the USSR or the Soviet Union, launched *Sputnik 1* in 1957 – the first man-made object to be put into orbit around the Earth. It was a simple ball-with-sticks-on device, but it was a great scientific achievement. Later, in 1961, Russian cosmonaut Yuri Gagarin amazed the world by becoming the first person in space. It was clear that Russia was well ahead in the Space Race. In 1961, the American President, John F. Kennedy, publicly pledged that the USA would land someone on the Moon before the end of the decade.

THE RACE HEATS UP

There were many attempts, by both the USA and the USSR, to get unmanned vehicles to the Moon. There were countless failures – rockets exploded on take-off or went completely off course – but there were also successes. Both countries managed to land probes on the surface of the Moon (crash-landed, mostly, but that was deliberate because they were designed to survive the impact). Thousands of pictures of the Moon's surface were beamed back to Earth and used to choose a place for a manned mission to land. The USA would not give up the race without a fight.

The Saturn V rocket blasts off!

THE APOLLO 11 MISSION

On 16th July 1969, huge crowds packed the roads, fields and beaches around the rocket launch site at Cape Canaveral, east of Orlando, Florida, while millions more sat glued to their TV screens. They waited to see the three-man space mission, *Apollo 11,* set off on a historic journey to land a tiny vehicle on the Moon with two men inside it.

That tiny vehicle was housed inside the tip of what looked like an enormous black-and-white bullet: a rocket called a *Saturn V*. Below the crew's small spaceship, the entire rocket was one giant fuel tank.

The astronauts, tightly strapped in, were Neil Armstrong, Edwin 'Buzz' Aldrin and Michael Collins, experienced military pilots who had spent years training for this day. Final checks were made, anticipation mounted and at around 9.30 a.m. *Apollo 11* finally blasted off, smoke and flames gushing beneath it as the rocket lifted and rose up, up, up into a clear blue sky.

One minute later, it was moving at around the speed of sound (1,192 kph or 741 mph).

Twelve minutes later, it entered Earth's orbit.

JOURNEY TO THE MOON

As fuel was used up, sections of the rocket were jettisoned and fell away. Eventually, all that was left shooting through space was the small, stubby Command Module attached nose-to-nose to the delicate-looking, spidery Lunar Module (called *Eagle*) that would eventually land on the Moon.

It took about three days for the men and their spaceship to travel the 384,000 kilometres (239,000 miles) to the Moon, and keeping on course was an extremely complicated mix of maths and engineering. At that time, even the most powerful computers on Earth could do little more than a modern pocket calculator. *Apollo 11*'s guidance computer had a total memory of 64 kilobytes – less than you would find in a kitchen appliance today. Imagine relying on a toaster to get you to the Moon!

On 19th July, the Command Module went into lunar orbit and circled the Moon thirty times, exactly as planned, while the astronauts kept a close eye on the landing site that had been chosen on the Sea of Tranquillity (not actually a sea but a suitably flat area, free of rocks which could cause damage). Everything had gone perfectly.

So far ...

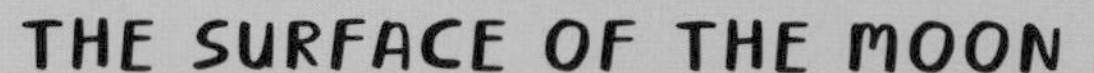

THE SURFACE OF THE MOON

On 20th July, Neil Armstrong and Buzz Aldrin crawled through a connecting tube into the *Eagle* lander while Michael Collins stayed behind to monitor the landing. With a clank, the *Eagle* separated and slowly began to descend towards the surface of the Moon.

Moments later, Armstrong and Aldrin suddenly realised their vehicle was passing landmarks on the Moon's surface about four seconds too early. This meant that the *Eagle* would overshoot its landing site by several kilometres. The navigation computer started raising alarms. As Armstrong peered out of the window, he realised the lander would hit a 100-metre crater surrounded by boulders if they didn't find a solution. Fast.

The astronauts, trained for such emergencies, quickly took control of the vehicle's guidance system. Aldrin called out data about their speed and distance from the Moon while Armstrong adjusted the computer accordingly. With only 25 seconds of fuel to spare, the *Eagle* touched down safely.

A few moments later, Mission Control on Earth heard: 'Houston, Tranquillity Base here. The *Eagle* has landed.'

The control room erupted with cheers!

ONE GIANT LEAP

Six and a half hours after landing, a hatch on the *Eagle*'s side slowly opened up. Neil Armstrong, moving carefully in a bulky white spacesuit, stepped on to the short ladder and climbed down to the Moon's surface. A TV camera attached to the landing vehicle transmitted the scene to hundreds of millions of people back on Earth.

Armstrong reached the ground and as he placed a foot on to the surface of the Moon he spoke one of the most momentous sentences in history: 'That's one small step for a man, one giant leap for mankind.'

For the two and a half hours, Armstrong and Aldrin explored the terrain of the Moon. They made notes, took photographs and dug soil samples, bouncing along in the low gravity and taking care not to slip on the loose, dusty lunar soil. They planted a US flag in the ground, which then got blown over when they took off for home! They left behind a few commemorative items, including a silicon disc containing messages from seventy-three world leaders.

THE JOURNEY HOME

The journey home took another three days. By then, the only part of the enormous *Saturn V* rocket remaining was a small, cone-shaped capsule. As it dropped down through Earth's atmosphere, its base was scorched by friction with the air. Three parachutes attached to its nose helped to slow it down as it splashed into the Pacific Ocean. The capsule bobbed around in the waves for an hour until a US military ship picked it up.

The successful return of the astronauts sparked celebrations everywhere! However, Armstrong, Collins and Aldrin had to put their celebrations on hold while they went into quarantine for three weeks! This was in case they'd brought back any unknown germs with them from space.

They emerged on 16th August to a rapturous welcome from the public. Parades in their honour were held in New York, Chicago and Los Angeles. They had done it!

Today, the *Apollo 11*'s splashdown capsule is on display in the Smithsonian Museum in Washington, DC. The base of the capsule still bears the pitted scorch marks of its descent through the upper atmosphere.

UNITED STATES

Neil Armstrong and Buzz Aldrin bounce around on the Moon's surface – they are the first people ever to set foot on it.

ANNIE EDSON TAYLOR

TEACHER AND DAREDEVIL

Feats of daring nearly all fall into the don't-try-this-at-home category, especially this one! Annie Edson Taylor, an American teacher, did something that nobody had ever attempted before. On 24th October 1901, she went over Niagara Falls in a barrel!

A DANGEROUS IDEA

After her husband was killed fighting in the American Civil War, Annie Taylor drifted around the USA getting steadily poorer. By 1900, she knew she needed to come up with a money-making idea or she would spend the rest of her life in poverty. Surely, she thought, a stunt as spectacular and dangerous as going over Niagara Falls would bring her fame and fortune ... ?

Annie Edson Taylor waves to the crowds before plunging over Niagara Falls.

Niagara Falls, on the border between Canada and the USA, is the most powerful waterfall in North America, with a vertical drop of over 50 metres. The barrel she used was a custom-built pickle barrel made of oak and iron, around 1.5 metres high, with a mattress lining the inside and 'Queen of the Mist' painted on the side. An anvil was sealed into the bottom of the barrel, so that the weight of it would make the barrel bob upright when it was in the water. Taylor tested the barrel a couple of days before the event by sending it over with a cat inside! Amazingly, the poor animal survived.

Taylor hired a manager to help her publicise the stunt and several thousand people turned up on the day to watch. Even with all those people, she had trouble getting anyone to help her because she was doing something very risky.

READY TO TAKE A TUMBLE

At 4.00 p.m. Taylor climbed into the barrel along with her lucky heart-shaped cushion. The lid was screwed down and a bicycle pump was used to compress the air inside. The barrel floated out into the middle of the river, a few hundred metres from the waterfall, and was then cut loose. There was no turning back now. The barrel, with Taylor inside, was pulled along, faster and faster, finally plunging over the edge of the Falls.

Onlookers lost sight of her for several minutes ...

At last, they caught sight of the barrel battling through the rapids at the foot of the Falls. Taylor was unhurt apart from a cut on her forehead – caused when she was hauled out. From the moment she was back on dry land, she vowed she'd never do it again. She later said, 'I would sooner walk up to the mouth of a cannon knowing it was going to blow me to pieces than make another trip over the Fall.'

Despite everything, Annie Taylor never made much money from her stunt. The newspapers were full of her story for a few days but it was soon forgotten. What little she made from recounting her experience went on chasing her manager, who had stolen her barrel and run off with it!

MIKE HORN

CONSERVATIONIST AND EXPLORER

Mike Horn, a conservationist and explorer born in South Africa, is said to have visited more of the Earth's surface than any other human being alive. The range of his expeditions and adventures is jaw-dropping ...

MIKE HORN
b. 1966

THE ENTIRE LENGTH OF THE AMAZON

His first major trip was down the entire length of the Amazon River in South America. From the Pacific coast of Peru, he climbed up into the Andes Mountains to the source of the river. He spent six months, on his own, following the Amazon for 7,000 kilometres (4,300 miles). He didn't take any food or water with him, finding food in the jungle and sleeping on the extremely dangerous riverbanks. He'd trained with the military in Brazil before he set out so he knew what was safe to eat and what river creatures might try to kill him, including alligators, various snakes, electric eels, bull sharks and piranhas. What's more, he swam all the way with the help of only a hydrospeed – a shaped board you hang on to, a bit like half a surfboard.

FIRST SOLO TRIP AROUND THE WORLD ALONG THE EQUATOR

Horn's 'Latitude Zero' voyage was the world's first solo trip around the world along the equator. As before, he was alone and had no engine-driven support. Leaving from Gabon in Africa, he travelled west by sail, bike, canoe and on foot. Circling the globe via oceans, deserts and jungles, he arrived back in Africa and walked across the continent. In the Democratic Republic of the Congo, rebel soldiers captured him, thinking he was a spy. He was put in front of a firing squad and only escaped at the last second when a local police officer intervened.

FIRST PERSON TO ROUND THE ARCTIC CIRCLE WITHOUT MOTORISED TRANSPORT

He made a similar, two-year-long trip, becoming the first person to travel around the Arctic Circle without motorised transport. His 20,000-kilometre (12,400-mile) journey took him through Greenland, Canada, Alaska, the Bering Strait and Siberia, pulling a Kevlar sled carrying 180 kilograms of equipment and food.

TO THE NORTH POLE IN TOTAL DARKNESS

In 2006, with Norwegian explorer Børge Ousland, he walked on skis from Cape Arktichesky in Russia to the North Pole in total darkness. For two months of the daylight-free Arctic winter, without even using dogs to pull their sleds, they crossed paper-thin ice and frequently had to swim through the freezing Arctic waters.

LONGEST SOLO NORTH-TO-SOUTH CROSSING OF ANTARCTICA

On top of all that, he completed the longest ever solo, unsupported north-to-south crossing of Antarctica, arriving at the South Pole on 9th January 2017. He covered a total distance of 5,100 kilometres (3,100 miles), using kites and skis, in 57 days.

Horn is also an accomplished mountaineer and a campaigner raising awareness of environmental issues. He drove through thirteen countries in 2015, from Switzerland to Pakistan, ending the journey with an attempt to climb the mountain K2. During his four-year Pangaea Expedition, he sailed around the world to set up an array of ecological projects and to highlight problems such as water pollution, melting ice caps and threats to biodiversity.

His family has been involved in his expeditions too: in 2005, his teenage daughters, Annika and Jessica, crossed the uninhabited Bylot Island (off Baffin Island in Canada) on skis and later became the youngest people ever to ski to the North Pole, in temperatures of around -35°C.

Mike Horn swims down the Amazon River with a hydrospeed.

BESSIE STRINGFIELD

MOTORCYCLIST AND DAREDEVIL

It's called the Wall of Death. Imagine a huge wooden cylinder, about 9 metres in diameter and about 6 metres high. You're inside it, with an audience looking down from the top. Your job is to ride a motorbike so *fast* that you can zoom round and round *on the vertical inside wall* of the cylinder, at a 90 degree angle. While you're up there, the audience will want to see you perform some tricks – balancing on the handlebars, kneeling on the saddle! Are you ready?

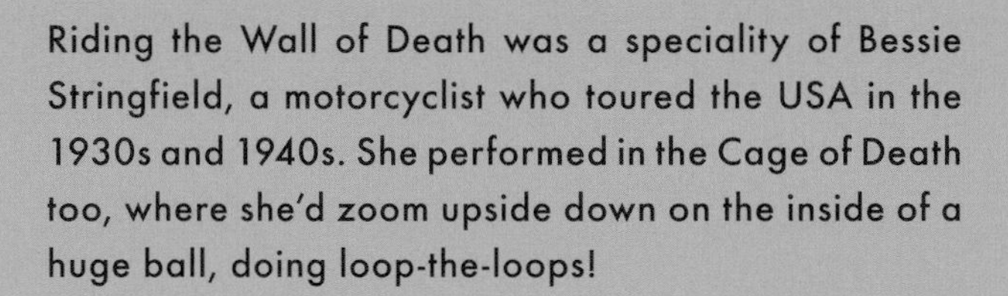

Riding the Wall of Death was a speciality of Bessie Stringfield, a motorcyclist who toured the USA in the 1930s and 1940s. She performed in the Cage of Death too, where she'd zoom upside down on the inside of a huge ball, doing loop-the-loops!

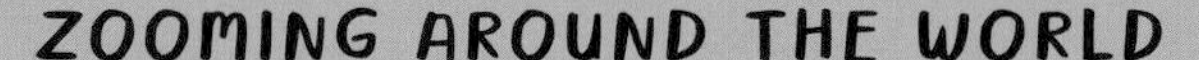

ZOOMING AROUND THE WORLD

In her teens, Springfield wanted a motorbike more than anything in the world, despite the fact she'd never even sat on one. She taught herself to ride on a 1928 Indian Scout model and in 1930, aged nineteen, she began over two decades of travelling on two wheels, mostly around the USA. She also rode across Brazil, the island of Haiti in the Caribbean and parts of Europe. She would decide on her next destination by opening up a map and flipping a coin – wherever it landed on the map, that was where she went!

In the 1930s, roads were still mostly dirt tracks – there were no such things as motorways, and no help available if you broke down in the middle of nowhere. You had to fix your own vehicle, which meant that long journeys could be tough.

Bessie Stringfield drives around the terrifying Wall of Death.

DEATH-DEFYING STUNTS

Stringfield supported herself by performing the Wall of Death and many other stunts at carnivals and big events. She soon became famous for it, not just because of her great skill but also because she was a black woman. Laws and attitudes at that time were disgracefully racist and crowds were astonished to see who was performing these amazing stunts.

She'd also take part in motorcycle races to earn cash – when she was allowed to. Before the start of one race, knowing that she'd be excluded, she disguised herself as a man. She lined up with all the male competitors, won the race, and only then took off her helmet to reveal her true identity. The crowd cheered but the race organisers wouldn't let her keep the prize money.

Bessie Stringfield's courage in the face of prejudice was extraordinary. While travelling, she'd often be refused a room at hotels, so she'd simply shrug her shoulders and sleep balancing on the back of her bike. One day, she was followed by a truck driver who deliberately forced her off the road. She had a proud resilience which told the world that nothing and nobody was going to put her off or get her down.

She preferred to ride a Harley-Davidson and owned twenty-seven of them over the years. She also got married and divorced six times and never lived anywhere for very long until she moved to Florida in the 1950s, where she was nicknamed 'Motorcycle Queen of Miami'. In old age, she ignored the advice of her doctor and kept on biking for as long as she could. She once summed herself up nicely when she said, 'What I did was fun and I loved it. I was never like anyone else.'

MERIWETHER LEWIS
SOLDIER AND EXPLORER

WILLIAM CLARK
SOLDIER AND EXPLORER

SACAGAWEA
NAVIGATOR

Sacagawea, Lewis and Clark trek across North America.

In the history of exploration, you can't avoid the fact that there's often a lot of fighting involved. One great expedition that was refreshingly different was made by the 'Corps of Discovery'. This was a group of volunteers, mostly from the US army, led by Captain Meriwether Lewis and Second Lieutenant William Clark.

The purpose of the expedition was to explore the area from St. Louis, south of the Great Lakes, north-west through what is now Montana and Idaho to the Pacific coast. A huge chunk of this region had just been bought from France in what was known as the Louisiana Purchase.

THE CORPS OF DISCOVERY

Their three-year journey was a peaceful one thanks almost entirely to one woman who went with them, a Native American called Sacagawea (which means 'bird woman'). Details of her life before and after the Lewis and Clark Expedition are sketchy, but she was a member of the Shoshone tribe and had been captured by their rivals, the Hidatsa, at around twelve years old.

When the Corps of Discovery met Sacagawea in 1804, just a few months into their journey, she was expecting her first baby and married to Toussaint Charbonneau, a French trader (although she was treated more like a slave than a wife). Sacagawea and Charbonneau joined the expedition to translate Native American languages into English.

CROSSING THE ROCKY MOUNTAINS

On their travels, Sacagawea helped negotiate trades for fresh supplies – and one of these negotiations really stood out. The Corps met some of her old Shoshone tribe and it turned out that the current Shoshone chief was her brother, whom she hadn't seen since being kidnapped all those years before at the age of twelve! The Shoshone provided Lewis and Clark with horses and guides to cross the Rocky Mountains.

Sacagawea was an all-important member of the expedition for other reasons too. Her presence when they met other Native Americans ensured these encounters were peaceful. The other Native Americans were inclined to trust the visitors (even though most of them had never seen a white-skinned person before), partly because Sacagawea was also Native American and partly because no tribe sent women out on war parties. This was especially true after Sacagawea's baby was born (a boy nicknamed Pomp, meaning 'first born') because children were even less likely to be included in hostilities.

It wasn't just peaceful negotiations that Sacagawea brought to the expedition. When the expedition ran dangerously short of food, Sacagawea showed the men how to find and cook camas roots and other edible plants. She also identified plants that could be used as medicines.

DISASTER ON THE MISSOURI RIVER

Sacagawea also saved the expedition from disaster on the upper Missouri River. The boat that she and Charbonneau were travelling in nearly tipped over in choppy waters. While others scrambled to shore, Sacagawea – with Pomp strapped to her back – calmly retrieved charts, scientific equipment and other vital supplies from the rushing water. She ensured that all their hard work was not lost and the group were able to continue on their travels.

The Lewis and Clark Expedition is a milestone in the history of the USA and Sacagawea helped establish peaceful relations between American settlers and Native Americans at a time when such meetings often ended in bloodshed. When she left the expedition in 1805, Charbonneau was paid just over $400 and 320 acres of land for his services. Sacagawea got nothing.

However, history has been kinder to her and given her the recognition she truly deserved. Over the years, she's been celebrated with statues, stamps and coins, been portrayed in films and music and had many things named after her (including a lake, a mountain and a US battleship!). In the early twentieth century, the US women's suffrage movement adopted her as a symbol of their cause.

Sacagawea saves
important charts and
equipment from the
choppy waters.

FRANCIS DRAKE

PRIVATEER

Francis Drake made an enormous impact on the Elizabethan world, but by modern standards his sense of right and wrong was awful! He conducted a one-man war against Spain, which made him a hero in the eyes of Elizabeth I's court and a bloodthirsty pirate in the eyes of the Spanish.

In 1572, Drake was hired as a privateer by Elizabeth I – which meant he had her permission to steal anything and kill anyone, as long as they were Spanish (Elizabeth I of England and Philip II of Spain were serious rivals). Drake returned from voyages to Spain's colonies in the Americas wounded but with heaps of stolen gold, which delighted the queen. However, Philip II was more than a little annoyed and offered a reward of 20,000 ducats (about £4 million in today's money) for Drake's capture or death.

AROUND THE WORLD

In 1577, Elizabeth sent Drake on his travels again, this time to raid Spanish settlements along the east coast of South America and then explore the coastline further on. Five ships under Drake's command crossed the Atlantic to Brazil then headed south, calling at ports along the way, all the while stockpiling loot.

Only Drake's ship, the *Golden Hind* (originally called the *Pelican*), made it around the lower tip of South America, and although it was relatively small it made rapid progress up the Pacific coast of South America. Here, Spanish towns and merchant ships were almost unguarded because they'd never had a hostile ship arrive in their waters before! Drake took advantage of their vulnerability and seized coins and jewels as well as bars of gold and silver.

The *Golden Hind* carried on plundering, sailing north and claiming California in the name of Queen Elizabeth I. The ship may have gone as far as Alaska before turning west across the Pacific, but we don't know for sure. Drake sailed through the East Indies and Indian Ocean before rounding the Cape of Good Hope and heading north again for Europe and home.

The ship arrived in Plymouth Harbour in the autumn of 1580, heaped with treasure and valuable spices. Drake had become the second person in history to sail around the world, after Portuguese navigator Ferdinand Magellan. The queen came on board his ship to personally welcome him back with a knighthood and a large amount of cash.

THE SPANISH ARMADA

By 1586, Philip II was itching for revenge. Drake was *still* plundering the American coasts. The Spanish prepared an armada, a mighty invasion fleet, but it was no match for Drake's, who, with two dozen English ships, sailed into the Spanish port of Cádiz and destroyed the Spanish vessels. Drake called this 'singeing the King of Spain's beard'.

But Philip would not give up and a year or so later in July 1588, 130 Spanish ships were sighted off the coast of Cornwall. The ships in Drake's fleet were faster and easier to steer but it took a series of scrappy battles – helped by bad weather – before the Spanish retreated with over a third of their ships lost.

It's said that Drake was playing bowls at Plymouth when the Armada was sighted. Cool as a cucumber, he stated there was plenty of time to defeat the Spanish and calmly finished his game before heading for his ship. The story is probably not true, but it's a good illustration of Drake's personality and his attitude toward his enemies.

Francis Drake is knighted aboard his ship after another fruitful voyage.

MARTHE CNOCKAERT

SPY

At the start of World War I in 1914, the German army invaded Belgium. The small town of Westrozebeke was burnt to the ground and among those made homeless was a young medical student called Marthe Cnockaert.

Cnockaert was bitterly opposed to the invasion, but she needed money to support herself and her family so she got a job at a German military hospital. She was so dedicated to caring for her patients, under terrible conditions, that the Germans awarded her the Iron Cross medal for bravery. At the time, being rewarded by her enemies didn't exactly fill her with pride, but

BECOMING A SPY

In 1915, Cnockaert was approached by an old family friend, Lucelle Deldonck. Deldonck revealed that she was now a spy for the British and wanted to know if Cnockaert would be interested in joining their undercover network. It was an opportunity too good to miss.

For the next two years, Cnockaert secretly gathered information about enemy plans, quietly passing it to the British and their allies at various local churches. She was in an ideal position to spy on the Germans – she could accidentally-on-purpose 'overhear' conversations while working at the hospital and also while helping out at her parents' café.

Her cover was so good that a neighbour called Otto, who assumed she was loyal to the Germans and had no idea she was spying for the British, offered her the chance to become a *German* agent! For a while, she played along and passed fake information on to Otto, to confuse the enemy. However, the moment he got suspicious she told British Intelligence about him ... and that was the end of Otto.

Marthe Cnockaert sneaks underground to set a trap.

Cnockaert's most daring mission was also to be her last. In 1916, she discovered an old sewer tunnel that led directly underneath an ammunition depot. In the dead of night, she and an agent codenamed 'Alphonse' crept along the tunnel and placed enough explosives to blow the German supplies sky high. Unfortunately, it wasn't only explosives Cnockaert left in the tunnel: she dropped her watch, upon which her initials were engraved. It was a clue that directly led back to her and she was soon caught by the German authorities.

Cnockaert was sentenced to death. However, the military discovered that she had received the Iron Cross and were reluctant to execute someone who'd been given such a high honour. They put her in prison instead.

After the war, following her release, Cnockaert was awarded many further honours for her courage from the British, the French and the Belgians. She went to live in Britain and, under the name Marthe McKenna, wrote a series of spy novels.

IBN BATTUTA

SCHOLAR AND EXPLORER

The Italian merchant Marco Polo is often thought of as the greatest traveller of medieval times, but a Moroccan scholar called Abu Abdullah Muhammad Ibn Battuta came along shortly after and made Polo's journeys look like a stroll around the park!

Over a period of nearly thirty years, Battuta covered around 121,000 kilometres (75,000 miles), visiting over forty countries and meeting more than sixty powerful rulers. His account of his travels, *A Gift to Those Who Contemplate the Wonders of Cities and the Marvels of Travelling*, is still a remarkable insight into the world as it was at that time.

HIS JOURNEY BEGINS

In 1325, aged twenty-one, Battuta set out on a hajj, the Muslim pilgrimage to the holy city of Mecca:

'I set out alone, without any travelling companions to keep up my spirits ... but a burning desire within me to reach my goal. I resolved to leave behind all those who were dear to me, and so I left my home like a young bird leaving its nest.'

Battuta didn't come home again for well over twenty years. That wasn't his original intention, but he quickly gained a thirst for exploration. The chance to see more of the great wide world was simply too good to resist!

Riding on a donkey, he set off from his home in Tangiers, Morocco. The hot, mountainous landscape he travelled through was full of bandits and cut-throats, so he soon joined a 'caravan' – a group of people all heading in the same direction, travelling together for safety. However, safety in numbers couldn't stop the fever that swept through Battuta's group. One traveller died while another had all of his gold stolen when he was too ill to notice. Battuta became so sick that he had to tie himself to his saddle so that he wouldn't fall off his donkey.

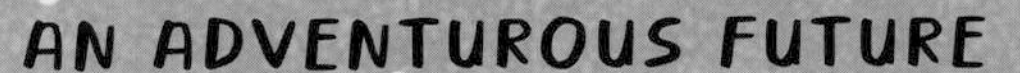

AN ADVENTUROUS FUTURE

When he arrived at Alexandria on the north coast of Egypt he had a strange dream:

'I was on the wing of an enormous bird, flying me towards Mecca. From there to Yemen, then eastwards and then turning towards the south, then flying far eastwards and finally landing in a dark and green country, where the giant bird left me.'

The holy man he was staying with at the time told him that the dream meant he would travel far and wide. Here was a sign, thought Battuta, that he should visit as many parts of the world as possible!

By this time, he was already making a name for himself. He'd studied law back home and his expertise could be traded for money or supplies. His studies also allowed him access to lots of educated people, which was most important to him because a hajj was intended as a chance to learn. The more he travelled, the more he found himself in demand as a scholar.

After visiting Cairo, Egypt, and travelling up the River Nile, he returned to his hajj and completed it in just under a year and a half. From that point on, he made a rule for himself 'never to travel any road a second time.'

Ibn Battuta travels from Morocco on a donkey.

Ibn Battuta greets Sultan Muhammad bin Tughluq in Delhi, India.

INDIA

Battuta arrived in Delhi, India, in 1334. The city was ruled by the richest man in the Muslim world, the Sultan Muhammad bin Tughluq, who gave Battuta a job as *qadi* (a judge).

Even by the standards of the Middle Ages, this sultan was a cruel and contrary ruler. He wrote poetry and heaped gold on scholars, but anyone who dared criticise him met a nasty death – often by being sliced in two or being thrown to elephants that had swords attached to their tusks. 'This king,' said Battuta, 'is of all men the most addicted to the making of gifts and the shedding of blood.'

Even so, Battuta served as *qadi* of Delhi for several years because it was an extremely well paid job. He even got married. In total, he married and divorced ten times during his travels!

After narrowly avoiding execution when he was suspected for a time of having associations with traitors to the sultan, Battuta was relieved to be commanded to become the sultan's ambassador to the emperor of China. The emperor had sent fifteen messengers to Delhi and Battuta was to accompany them home, taking a huge pile of gifts along with him.

Battuta's expedition, escorted by one thousand soldiers, was a complete disaster. On their way to the coast they were attacked by three thousand rebels. His escort of soldiers scattered and Battuta spent a week hiding in a swamp and was left with nothing but his trousers! When they finally regrouped and boarded a ship for China, it sank in a storm! Battuta, realising he'd be put to death if he returned to Delhi, took refuge in the Maldive Islands in the Indian Ocean, becoming *qadi* to their queen.

CHINA

Resuming his journey as a wandering scholar, Battuta arrived at Quanzhou on China's east coast in 1345. He saw local artists making drawings of all newly-arrived foreigners for security purposes, just like modern airports photographing arrivals!

China gave Battuta a culture shock. This was the first time he'd been somewhere that wasn't Muslim, and at first he found Chinese dress, food and behaviour deeply shocking.

However, he soon came to appreciate things like Chinese silk and porcelain, as well as the country's landscape. He marvelled at the sights and sounds of Hangzhou, then the largest city in the world. In the end, he called China 'the safest and best country for the traveller'.

He returned home for good in 1354. It was the ruler of Morocco, Abu Inan Faris, who suggested he write down the story of his travels. Battuta never actually took any notes during his years of travelling, so his memories may not always have been accurate.

After the book was finished, Battuta all but vanished from history. We know he was a judge in Morocco and died around 1368, but that's about it. Unlike many great voyagers of history, Ibn Battuta travelled purely for the joy of wandering and the chance to learn. He went wherever he felt like going, often changing his mind at the last minute. He travelled at whatever speed suited him and when he found somewhere interesting he stayed there a while. You can tell he wasn't usually heading in any particular direction by the way a map of his travels weaves around here, there and everywhere!

'Travel gives you a hundred roads to adventure and gives wing to your heart. It leaves you speechless with wonder, then turns you into a storyteller.'

JEANNE D'ARC (ALSO KNOWN AS JOAN OF ARC)

MILITARY HEROINE

JEANNE D'ARC
1412–1431

Jeanne d'Arc leads the charge for France.

In January 1431, in the castle at Rouen in France, a trial began. The accused was facing seventy mostly made-up charges, including witchcraft, and her captors were determined to see her burn at the stake. Over the previous two years, she had become a living symbol of unity and liberation for the French, someone who'd inspired victory almost by the sheer force of her personality. She was a teenager from a peasant family, unable to read or write, and her name was Jeanne d'Arc.

England's King Henry V had defeated the French at the Battle of Agincourt when Jeanne was two years old and as a result the English occupied a large chunk of northern France. The French were divided and demoralised under their uncrowned King Charles VII.

JEANNE HAS A VISION

Jeanne was a deeply religious girl and claimed to have spiritual visions. These visions drove her to demand an audience with Charles so passionately that, in the end, a meeting was grudgingly allowed. At their meeting, she told Charles that her destiny was to boot the English out of France and see him crowned king. At this point Charles and his court were desperate for anything that might help defeat the invaders, so they decided to put Jeanne's claims to the test.

At that time, women of any age, let alone sixteen-year-old girls, never took part in fighting wars and they certainly never commanded armies. But Jeanne wasn't about to let any of that nonsense stand in her way and, wearing borrowed armour and flying a banner of her own design, she led a French army to the city of Orléans, which was surrounded by English soldiers. Before their arrival she sent a letter to the English military leaders at Orléans basically telling them to leave the city before she got there or she'd make them leave. The English just sniggered and shook their heads.

VICTORY FOR THE FRENCH

A siege of the city had been in place for six months. After Jeanne arrived, it was over in nine days. A series of fierce battles swept the English aside, showing the whole of France that the English weren't anywhere near as invincible as they'd once seemed. It was the turning point in the war. Jeanne was dubbed the 'Maid of Orléans' and quickly became the Middle Ages' equivalent of a superhero, inspiring the French forces to fight on! Further battles brought more victories and, as she'd predicted, Charles was soon crowned king.

CAPTURE AND TRIAL

However, Jeanne wasn't invincible – she was captured by some of Charles's enemies in 1430 and sold to the English, who imprisoned her at Rouen. Charles, for whom she'd done so much, made no attempt whatsoever to rescue her. She was questioned (bullied would be a better word) for three months and almost every word was written down, which is the reason we know so much about Jeanne d'Arc's life.

At first, the trial was held in public – the English were keen to make an example of Jeanne and show the French who was boss. However, Jeanne faced her accusers so calmly and ran rings around their arguments so cleverly that the public stayed firmly on her side and were soon excluded. The authorities were never going to let her win. It's said that over ten thousand people attended her execution on 30th May 1431. She was nineteen years old.

Among true-life tales of guts, determination and triumph, few are as dramatic as Jeanne d'Arc's. Her immense courage and strength of character, both in battle and throughout her trial, have secured her place in history and today she is the patron saint of France.

ROALD AMUNDSEN
ROBERT SCOTT

POLAR EXPLORERS

Captain Cook had mapped the edges of Antarctica and, by the second half of the 1800s, there was an international scramble to explore and scientifically examine the region. The most sought-after goal of all was to reach the South Pole and in the early years of the twentieth century, Roald Amundsen and Robert Scott took on the challenge. The race was on!

ROALD AMUNDSEN
1872–1928

ROALD AMUNDSEN

Roald Amundsen came from a Norwegian seafaring family. He had a lifelong ambition to be a polar explorer and in 1897 he had his first experience of Antarctica as first mate on a Belgian expedition. However, their ship got trapped in ice for several months, leading to severe malnutrition among the crew. Here, Amundsen learned important lessons about being properly prepared for such a long, gruelling journey – lessons that would help him in the future.

ROBERT SCOTT

Captain Scott, a Royal Navy officer from Plymouth, became an explorer almost by accident. He bumped into an old friend who was planning a scientific trip to Antarctica and volunteered to lead it! The 'Discovery Expedition' of 1901–1904 mapped many geographical features of Antarctica, including the region's only snow-free valleys and the Polar Plateau, on which the South Pole sits.

The expedition got to within 850 kilometres (530 miles) of the pole. They might have got closer but were forced to turn back due to injuries, malnutrition and snow-blindness (temporary but painful loss of sight caused by light reflecting off snow).

ROBERT SCOTT
1868–1912

THE EXPEDITIONS

Scientific exploration is an expensive business and Amundsen got himself into enormous debt in order to keep going. By the time he'd organised his own expedition, ten major voyages had already surveyed Antarctica. If his expedition were not a big success he'd be ruined. This is why, at the last minute, Amundsen made a sudden change of plan.

Plan A had been to reach the North Pole, but news arrived in 1909 that two American expeditions had got there first. Amundsen, knowing his own trip there would now seem pointless, switched to Plan B – reaching the South Pole. His rival, Captain Scott, was setting out for the South Pole too, so without telling his crew he decided to head in the opposite direction and try to beat Scott to it. He left Norway in August 1910.

Meanwhile, Scott had 8,000 volunteers lining up to join his 'Terra Nova' expedition. When it stopped off at South Africa in October 1910, Scott found a message from Amundsen waiting for him. It said, 'Beg to inform you ... proceeding Antarctic – Amundsen.' In other words: *ha, ha I'm ahead of you.*

The team skis through the harsh Antarctic landscape.

THE RACE

Amundsen landed at the Bay of Whales in Antarctica at the start of 1911. It took several more months to run 'mini-expeditions', which placed food and other essentials along the route they'd take to the South Pole. Then they waited out the icy darkness of the winter and finally set off in October 1911, in temperatures of -27°C.

Scott's ship nearly sank in a huge storm and then got trapped in ice for twenty days. They still managed to reach Antarctica at about the same time as Amundsen and landed at Cape Evans, 320 kilometres (200 miles) west of the Bay of Whales. Scott too made preparations and wintered at base camp, then was ready to depart for the pole on 1st November 1911.

Despite the lengthy plans made by both expeditions, Amundsen's crew was better supplied and better organised ...

- Amundsen copied the Inuit people of the Arctic and used fur skins for warmth instead of the heavy woollen clothes worn by Scott.
- Amundsen's crew used skis while Scott's walked.
- Scott's team had nowhere near enough food to keep them going. They steadily weakened and lost weight throughout the journey.
- Perhaps most important of all, Amundsen used strong North Greenland dogs to pull loads and knew exactly how to handle them. Scott made the serious mistake of relying on Siberian ponies, which weren't suited to polar conditions. He also used motorised sledges, which were still experimental - one of them fell through the ice and was lost as it was being unloaded from the ship.

On the afternoon of 14th December 1911, Amundsen and a three-man crew at long last planted the Norwegian flag at the South Pole – and won the race!

They spent three days checking and re-checking that they'd reached the correct spot – Amundsen didn't want there to be any possible doubt about their achievement. Before heading back, they left a tent with some equipment for Scott inside and a letter detailing their journey in case they themselves didn't make it back.

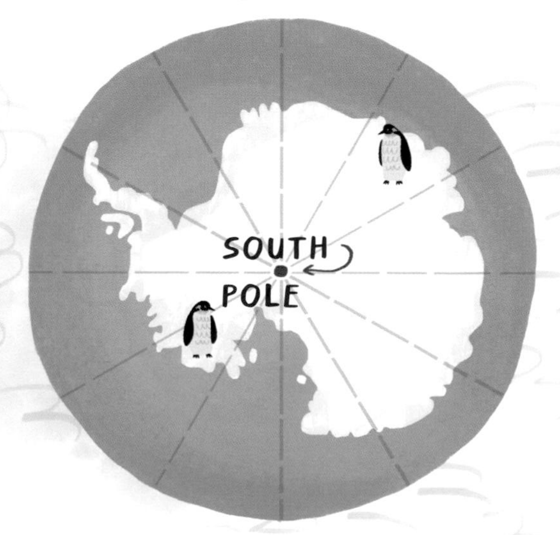

THE JOURNEY HOME

Scott missed them by just over a month. His bitter disappointment showed in his diary, where he wrote, 'Great God! This is an awful place.' Already hungry and exhausted, they started the 1,300-kilometre (800-mile) walk back to base camp.

Amundsen's group had a relatively uneventful journey home. Meanwhile, Scott's five-man team met unexpectedly bad weather and temperatures of -40°C. On the Beardmore Glacier, they lost their way and spent two days trying to work out which direction was the right one. Progress slowed and there were regular injuries from falls. Frostbite badly affected all of them, but particularly Captain Lawrence Oates. He famously left the tent they were huddled in, saying, 'I am just going outside and may be some time.' He never returned. None of them survived. Scott and the last members of his team froze to death just a few miles short of one of the supply dumps they'd set up months earlier.

Meanwhile, Amundsen got back to his ship in January 1912, his crew safe and sound. Of the fifty-two dogs that had started the journey, eleven had survived (some of them, as was planned, were eaten along the way). Getting to the South Pole and back, travelling a distance of over 3,000 kilometres (1,850 miles), had taken 99 days.

Amundsen plants the Norwegian flag at the South Pole.

CHING SHIH

PIRATE

Ching Shih rose from poverty to become one of the most fearsome pirates in history, and definitely one of the richest. Born Shi Xiang Gu, Ching Shih (meaning 'Ching's widow') married the notorious pirate Ching Yi in 1801. She agreed to the marriage on the condition that she would be her husband's equal and have her fair share of the loot. She took to piracy like a duck to water.

Ching Shih surrounded by her loot after another successful adventure.

THE RED FLAG FLEET

After Ching Yi's death in 1807, Ching Shih seized command of his Red Flag Fleet. This was a group of 300 pirate junks (traditional Chinese sailing ships) that had joined forces to form one enormous band of raiders. At the height of Ching Shih's power, the fleet consisted of around 1,800 boats, with around 80,000 pirates! The Red Flag Fleet became the most feared on the high seas and Ching Shih was known as 'The Terror of South China'. The pirates sailed up and down the Chinese coast, stealing from villages and raiding merchant ships. They were as close to invincible as it's possible to get!

Ching Shih expected her pirates to abide by an ultra-tough set of rules, which were written out and pinned up on every ship in the fleet. Disobey an order – death. Attack without permission – death. Leave your post while on duty – first time, you lose your ears, second time, death. The code of conduct was very, very strict. Individual pirates were allowed to keep some of the loot they took, but any disrespect shown to women would result in a punishment that made death look like a holiday!

THE END OF HER REIGN

The Chinese government were determined to put a stop to Ching Shih's piracy, so they set a trap. The entire Chinese navy blocked off a bay where the Red Flag Fleet was anchored and sent in junks that were on fire and loaded with explosives in Ching Shih's direction.

The Chinese navy was no match for Ching Shih and her fearsome crew. Not only did the pirates put out the flames, but they also captured the junks and kept them for themselves – making their fleet even bigger! The navy attacked but once again Ching Shih showed them who was in charge. She defeated the navy and succeeded in taking a further sixty-three ships from them.

The Chinese forces were so badly damaged that they had to use little fishing boats afterwards. It was clear they needed assistance to conquer Ching Shih and her powerful band of pirates. China called on warships from Portugal to help battle the Red Flag Fleet, but they too were defeated by the pirates, and so were warships from Britain's East India Company. Ching Shih ruled the South China Sea!

But Ching Shih was smart enough to realise that this situation couldn't last. The government wouldn't give up until the Red Flag Fleet was destroyed. In 1810, she decided to call it a day, but only if a peace deal was agreed on her terms. Almost all of her pirates escaped punishment, and they were even allowed to keep their loot! Ching Shih quietly retired and lived out the rest of her life as a very wealthy woman.

PHILIPPE PETIT

HIGH-WIRE ARTIST

Philippe Petit, a high-wire artist from France, caused a sensation when he walked on a tightrope over Notre Dame cathedral in Paris in 1971. Two years later, he did the same thing at the Sydney Harbour Bridge in Australia. By 1974, he was ready for what he called *'le coup'*, the greatest performance of his career.

He'd been thinking about it ever since his visit to the dentist in 1968. In a magazine in the waiting room, he read about the planned construction of the World Trade Center in New York, USA ... and an idea for something spectacular popped into his head ...

A WALK ON A TIGHTROPE

Shortly after 7.00 a.m. on Wednesday, 7th August 1974, crowds of New Yorkers began to gather around the base of the Twin Towers – two skyscrapers which made up the World Trade Center. With curiosity, they looked up to where, high above them, Petit was about to step out on to a steel cable weighing 200 kilograms, stretched from the roof of one of the towers across a 42-metre gap to the other. Petit had no safety devices. If he fell, nothing could stop him hitting the ground 411 metres below.

The moment had come. Petit put one foot out ...

For forty-five minutes, Petit walked back and forth – eight times in all, keeping his balance with the help of a specially made 8-metre-long pole. He didn't just walk either, he also danced, lay down flat and even knelt to salute the crowd, whose distant cheers he could hear drifting up to him.

The crowd loved the performance. The police didn't. What Petit was doing was illegal, so he and the team of friends who'd helped him were in serious trouble.

A SECRET PLAN

The event had been planned for many months. All sorts of practical issues had to be considered: how to allow for the slight sway of the buildings in the wind, how slippery the cable might get at that height, how to get the cable and all the other heavy equipment up to the roof without being spotted.

Petit and his team had made over 200 undercover visits to the World Trade Center while it was still under construction, to help them work out how to do it. They had posed as builders, office workers, photographers, architects and journalists to gain access to different parts of the buildings. On the night of 6th August 1974, they hid themselves and their equipment high up inside one of the towers and waited until morning.

The cable was too heavy to be thrown from one roof to the other. An arrow was fired across the gap, attached to a fishing line. The line was tied to a string, the string to a rope and so on, until the thick cable could be pulled into place and anchored with supports, like a tent being held down with guy ropes.

AN UNFORGETTABLE PERFORMANCE

After Petit was arrested, the authorities decided he and his friends had done the city a favour. Before this daring high-wire stunt, many New Yorkers had thought the World Trade Center was too big and ugly. Afterwards, everyone was talking about it! The charges against Petit were dropped, provided he performed a free high-wire show for the city's children.

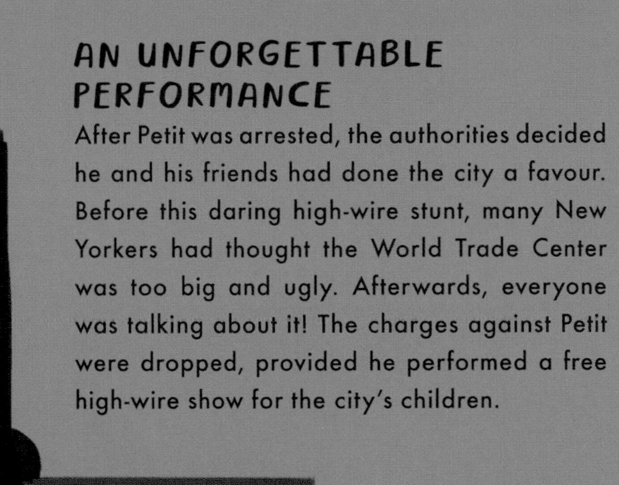

Philippe Petit makes a daring walk between the Twin Towers.

NELLIE BLY

JOURNALIST AND GLOBAL EXPLORER

In 1882, the *Pittsburgh Dispatch* newspaper ran an article headlined 'What Girls Are Good For'. According to this article, the answer was: staying at home in the kitchen. The editor got a furious letter from an eighteen-year-old reader called Elizabeth Cochrane, who gave the article such a well-written shouting down for being absolute rubbish that the editor offered her a job.

NELLIE BLY
1864–1922

Under the pen name Nellie Bly, Cochrane began a very successful career as a journalist. She became famous for her daring undercover reports exposing injustice, but hit the headlines herself in 1889 when she was working for the *New York World*.

ROUND THE WORLD WITH NELLIE

Jules Verne's adventure story *Around the World in Eighty Days* was a popular hit, so Bly suggested she should make a similar trip and try to beat the fictional character Phileas Fogg's record. Her boss refused, saying that no woman could possibly undertake such a journey on her own. Besides, women took so much luggage with them when they travelled that she'd need an ocean liner just for all her hat boxes.

It's not hard to imagine the look on Bly's face. 'Fine,' she said. 'Send a man. I'll go anyway and I'll beat him to the finish line.'

Bly was so headstrong and determined that her boss had no choice but to give in.

HER ADVENTURE STARTS

Bly set off from New Jersey, travelling east across the Atlantic. All she had with her were the clothes she was wearing, an overcoat, £200 and a small bag containing underwear and toiletries. The *New York World* carried daily features about her progress – they even ran a competition to guess the exact moment of her return.

She travelled mostly by steamship and railway, but also used everything from rickshaws and sampans to horses and donkeys. She braved monsoons in Asia, visited a Chinese leper colony and got a pet monkey in Singapore.

It was only when she got to Hong Kong that she discovered she had a rival. Keen to grab some round-the-world publicity for themselves, *Cosmopolitan* magazine had sent one of their own reporters, Elizabeth Bisland, in the opposite direction on the same day Bly left America! Bisland came close to beating Bly, but was held back by bad weather in the Atlantic.

A TRIUMPHANT RETURN

Greeted by brass bands and fireworks, Nellie Bly arrived back in New York at 3.51 p.m. on 25th January 1890. She'd travelled 40,071 kilometres (24,899 miles) around the world in exactly 72 days, 6 hours, 11 minutes and 14 seconds – beating Phileas Fogg's fictional record! Readers everywhere had followed her adventures – she was so famous that there were Nellie Bly trading cards and a 'Round the World with Nellie Bly' board game. Among the things named after her were a hotel, a train and a racehorse. She wrote a book about her journey and continued her investigative journalism. She became a war reporter in Europe during World War I and when she died in 1922, she was hailed as simply 'the best reporter in America'.

Nellie Bly returns to New York after an amazing round-the-world trip.

AUGUSTE PICCARD

PHYSICIST AND EXPLORER

JACQUES PICCARD

OCEANOGRAPHER

BERTRAND PICCARD

BALLOONIST

Most great pioneers tend to be one of a kind but the Piccards from Switzerland are a *family* of prominent scientists, explorers and inventors whose achievements span at least three generations.

AUGUSTE PICCARD ...

... was a professor of physics in Brussels, Belgium. He wanted to study cosmic rays in the Earth's upper atmosphere, about 16 kilometres (10 miles) off the ground. Nobody had ever reached anywhere near that height before, mostly because the human body needs normal, everyday air pressure to survive. The higher up you go, the thinner the air gets and the harder it becomes to breathe.

AUGUSTE PICCARD
1884–1962

Piccard's solution to this problem was to invent a ball-shaped aluminium pod about 1.8 metres across. It was built by a factory that usually made metal beer caskets and it was just big enough for Piccard and his assistant to squeeze into. The pod was airtight, with the air inside kept at normal pressure so they could still breathe at high altitude despite the thinning atmosphere outside. Passenger aircraft today work on exactly the same idea – that's why their doors and windows have to be kept tightly sealed!

READY FOR LIFT OFF

The pod took off on 27th April 1931, tied beneath a very tall, thin yellow hydrogen balloon. It wasn't a smooth flight: Piccard was still carrying out safety checks when the balloon launched too early, the pod sprang a leak which had to be hurriedly patched with cotton soaked in grease and the descent back to ground level went wrong and left the balloon floating across Europe with its oxygen tanks rapidly emptying. It finally landed on a glacier in the Alps, with barely one hour of air left.

Despite the difficulties, Piccard's balloon reached a record-breaking height of 15,781 metres and returned with lots of valuable scientific data. At that height, the curvature of the planet was visible – the first time any human being had seen it! Piccard went on to make twenty-seven balloon flights in all, reaching a final height of 23 kilometres (14 miles).

GOING DOWN ...

Auguste Piccard soon realised that the operating principle of his pod – keeping air at 'normal' pressure inside a sealed container – could be applied in the opposite direction: travelling down into the deepest parts of the oceans. In 1937, he designed what he called a bathyscaphe, a steel vessel (a bit like a submarine) built to withstand the intense water pressure deep under the surface. The bathyscaphe was gradually redesigned and improved upon over the next few years. Its greatest journey was made thanks to Auguste's son, Jacques.

Auguste Piccard and his assistant squeeze into a pod ready to travel upwards.

JACQUES PICCARD ...

... was an engineer and oceanographer. He helped his dad develop the bathyscaphe, *Trieste*, and in it the two of them dived to a depth of over 3,000 metres off the coast of Italy in 1953. Then, joining forces with the US Navy, Jacques undertook a journey every bit as daring and record-breaking as his father's – he took a trip down to the deepest point of the deepest waters on Earth!

THE CHALLENGER DEEP

The Mariana Trench is in the Pacific Ocean, north of Australia, between Japan and New Guinea. It's a crescent-shaped tear in the ocean floor and the deepest part of the trench is a narrow valley called the Challenger Deep, almost 11 kilometres (nearly 7 miles) down. If you dropped Mount Everest into it, the tip of the mountain would still be 1.6 kilometres (1 mile) underwater. The water pressure down there is about 1,086 bars – that's like having fifty or sixty airliners piled on top of you!

On 23rd January 1960, Jacques Piccard and Lieutenant Don Walsh took the *Trieste* down into the Challenger Deep. The descent took almost five hours. Sunlight is only visible underwater to a depth of about 1,000 metres so after that they had to rely on a powerful light fixed to the outside of the bathyscaphe. All went well until around 9,000 metres underwater when they heard a sudden, loud crack. The whole vessel shook and the two men had to decide quickly what to do next ...

Jacques Piccard looks out at the wonders of the deep.

AT THE VERY BOTTOM

They continued, dropping deeper into the ice-cold, pitch-black water. They reached the bottom just after 1.00 p.m., the first humans to land there. Visibility was very limited because of the oozy mud that the landing had stirred up, but they saw glimpses of sea creatures moving around. Until that moment, it was thought that the intense pressure would make life down there impossible. We've since learned that quite a lot of things can live at that depth!

The *Trieste* only spent twenty minutes on the ocean floor. The loud crack had been one of the 19-centimetre-thick outer windows splitting and it would be dangerous to stay any longer.

The discovery of life in the Challenger Deep had an important environmental impact: the dumping of nuclear waste in deep ocean locations was banned. In later years, ecological issues would come to be a concern of Jacques's son, Bertrand.

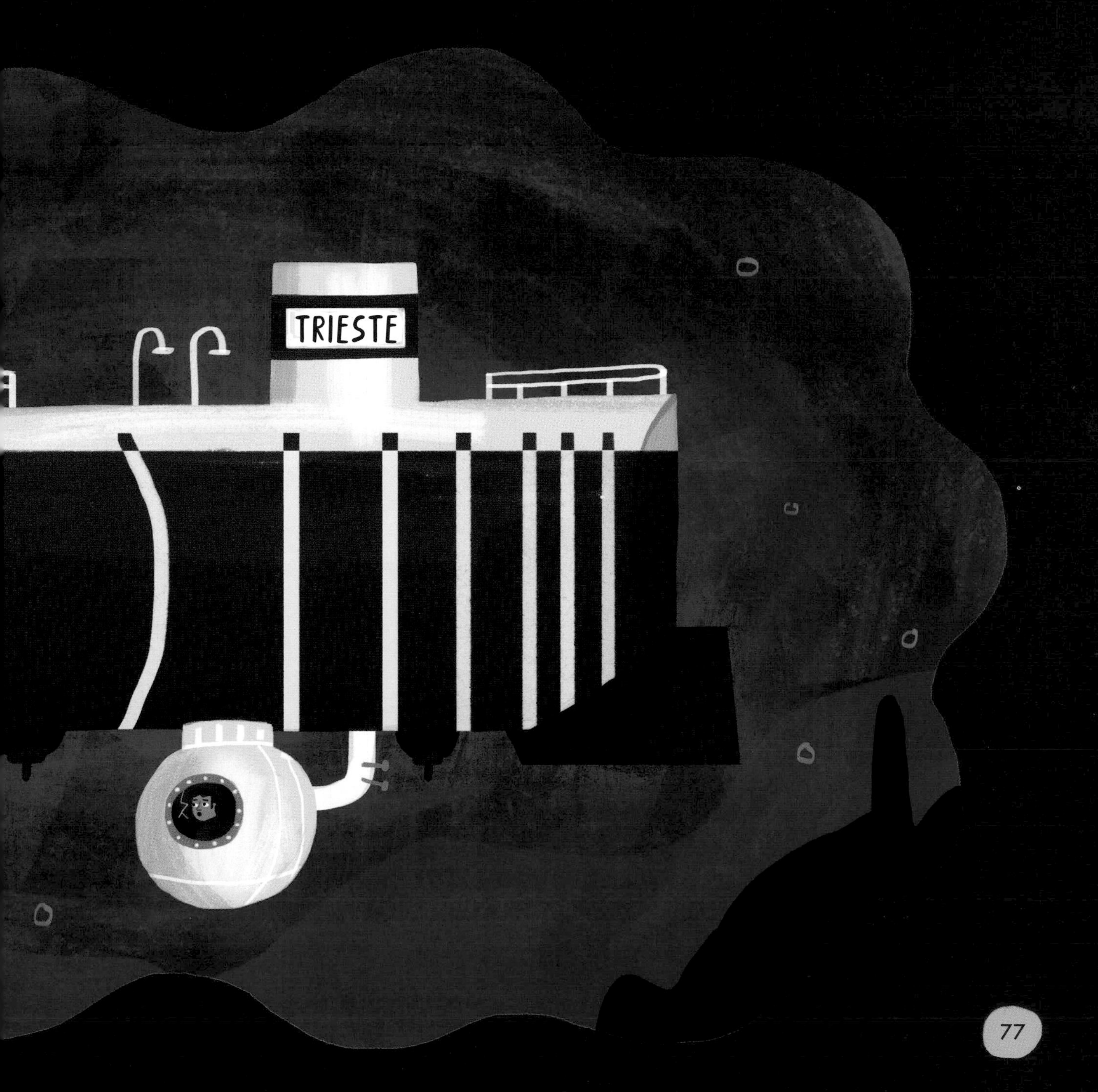

BERTRAND PICCARD ...

... followed in his grandfather's footsteps by taking to the air. In the 1970s, he pioneered hang-gliding and microlight flying in Europe (microlights are very small aircraft, a bit like hang-gliders with engines) but he's best known for yet another Piccard adventure: the first non-stop balloon flight around the world.

BERTRAND PICCARD
b. 1958

UP, UP AND AWAY

Several attempts at such a flight were made in the 1990s. In March 1999, Piccard and his co-pilot, Brian Jones, took off from Switzerland, on their third attempt, aboard their balloon *Breitling Orbiter 3*, a 55-metre-high update of Auguste's original design.

With the help of weather experts on the ground, they used jet streams (high-speed winds) to keep them moving for 19 days, 21 hours and 47 minutes. Despite being heated, the flight cabin sometimes got so cold at night – because they were so high up – that Piccard and Jones had to chip ice off delicate electronics fixed to the cabin walls. They landed in Egypt, not far from the pyramids, having circled the globe in the longest un-refuelled flight in history.

THE *SOLAR IMPULSE*

Bertrand Piccard and Swiss engineer André Borschberg were behind the *Solar Impulse* project, which aimed to show the benefits and possibilities of renewable energy by creating a solar-powered aircraft that could make a trip like Piccard's balloon trip.

The zero-emission, totally unfuelled *Solar Impulse II* was completed in 2014. Piloted by Piccard and Borschberg in turn, it achieved the first solar-powered, round-the-world voyage in a series of flights in 2015 and 2016.

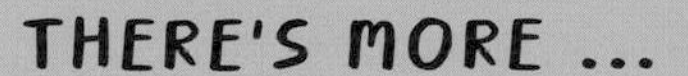

THERE'S MORE ...

Other members of the Piccard family took to the skies as well: Auguste's twin brother, Jean Felix, and sister-in-law, Jeannette, were high-altitude balloonists too. Their son Don Piccard flew a balloon (along with his mum) to the edge of space and founded the Balloon Club of America.

Bertrand Piccard flies the first solar-powered plane around the world.

MARTIN JOHNSON
OSA LEIGHTY

DOCUMENTARY FILM-MAKERS

Today, TV documentaries about far-flung places are easily available, making animal species and scenes of other cultures from around the world a familiar sight. However, in the first half of the twentieth century, seeing moving pictures of creatures and people from remote places was completely new and exciting. Martin and Osa Johnson from Kansas, USA, made some of the first natural history movies and popularised the genre.

Martin and Osa were huge celebrities and were something of a cross between Indiana Jones and David Attenborough! They recorded every aspect of their travels, aiming to preserve information about people and wildlife for future generations, and bringing the sights and sounds of far-off places, especially Africa, to North American and European audiences for the first time.

SOUTH PACIFIC VOYAGES

They made lots of trips over the years, resulting in over twenty movies as well as several books and countless lecture tours. On their first expedition in 1917, they travelled nearly 29,000 kilometres (18,000 miles) by sailing ship and canoe around what's now called Melanesia in the South Pacific (New Guinea, the Solomon Islands and Fiji). They contacted and lived with local people, in this case the Big Nambas tribes on the island of Vanuatu – people who were known for being cannibals, eating their defeated enemies! They were held captive for a while but were rescued by a British patrol boat. However, this encounter with danger didn't put them off and they returned to the tribe on their next voyage and were greeted like old friends!

SILENT FILMS

Some of the (silent) film and photos the Johnsons took of native peoples in Africa and the South Pacific were the very first images of these peoples seen outside their homelands. They also took the first images of gorillas in their natural habitat and, once film with sound was invented, they were the first to record jungle noises on location. After they'd both learned to fly a plane in 1932, they pioneered filming large animal herds from the air.

Life on film-safari could be tough. In those days, there were no flights to anywhere the Johnsons wanted to go and nowhere to get food or equipment once they got there. Looking after the film they took was a constant problem: these were the early years of cinema, when moving pictures were captured on strips of delicate plastic, which then had to be 'developed' using chemicals. In jungle conditions, film could easily be ruined by heat, moisture or even by fungus growing on it!

Given their efforts to educate and record, it's very hard to understand why the Johnsons were also hunters. Killing animals for sport horrifies many of us today, but attitudes to nature were very different in the past. On the other hand, Johnson movies such as *Across the World with Mr & Mrs Johnson* (1930) and *Wings over Africa* (1934) inspired millions to travel and greatly increased awareness of the natural world, which in turn sparked the far more respectful approach to nature that we have today!

Martin Johnson and Osa Leighty capture the wonders of wildlife on film.

HENRY 'BOX' BROWN

INVENTIVE ESCAPEE

Henry Brown, along with his wife and three children, were all born into slavery. Despite promises from his 'owner' that the family wouldn't ever be split up, he discovered one morning during the American Civil War that all four of them were being sold that same day. His family were sent to North Carolina, USA, along with 350 other slaves. All Brown could do was watch helplessly as they were taken away in chains. He never saw them again. His 'owner' only shrugged and said, 'You can get another wife.'

Grief-stricken and broken-hearted, Brown resolved to escape. With the help of a couple of friends who had already found freedom, a few discreet enquiries were made about what postal address to use to send something to the abolitionists (those who wanted to end slavery) in Pennsylvania.

THE PLAN IN ACTION

On 29th March 1849, Brown deliberately burnt his hand with acid so he could get out of work. Away from his master's prying eyes, his friends sealed him into a wooden packing crate that was 91 centimetres long, 61 centimetres wide and 81 centimetres deep, using nails and leather straps. The box was lined with a thin woollen fabric and had one small hole for air. It was stamped with the words 'Dry Goods' and was addressed to the offices of the Philadelphia Anti-Slavery Society.

Henry Brown spent the next twenty-seven hours squashed tightly into that box. All he had with him was a small container of water and a few biscuits. Despite the fact that 'This Side Up – With Care' was painted in big letters on the side, the box was hauled and tipped in every direction all over the place. Brown, unable to move at all, spent hours upside down. This can easily cause death because it can burst blood vessels in your brain or stop you from breathing. However, Brown was saved by chance when two postal workers turned the box back on its side so they could sit on it.

Henry 'Box' Brown arrives safely in Philadelphia.

A SPECIAL DELIVERY

The box arrived in Philadelphia the following day. It had been carried over 400 kilometres (250 miles) by wagon, railway and steamboat.

Four members of the Society, warned that Henry Brown was on the way, had gathered to receive their special delivery and opened it up at once. Out popped Brown with a cheery 'How do you do, gentlemen?' Then he burst into song!

Brown's amazing escape quickly made him famous, and got him his nickname 'Box' Brown. He became a campaigner for the abolitionist movement but after the Fugitive Slave Law was passed in 1850, it was very difficult for Brown to stay in the USA. He and his story were too well known. He moved to the UK in 1851 and lived in Manchester.

When asked why he'd done something so drastic and risky, he would reply, 'If you have never been deprived of your liberty, as I was, you cannot realise the power of that hope of freedom.'

KAREN DARKE

PARALYMPIAN AND EXPLORER

Karen Darke, from Halifax, UK, has what she calls 'an adventurous gene'. At the age of sixteen, she saw a poster at school advertising an expedition to China by the Yorkshire Schools Exploring Society. She spent a year raising money to afford the trip, which sparked her passion for adventure and learning about other cultures.

KAREN DARKE
b. 1971

Darke also became a keen runner and climber, but a fall while scaling a cliff in 1992 broke her back and left her paralysed from the waist down. Her resilience and determination meant that she was absolutely going to continue doing the things she loved!

THE PARALYMPICS

Switching from running to para-cycling, Darke qualified for the London 2012 British Paralympic team and won the silver medal in the 16-kilometre women's road time trial H1-2. At the Rio games in 2016, she beat seven other athletes to take the gold medal in the same event.

Away from the track, Darke has been on jaw-dropping adventures and expeditions. She has climbed mountains around the world – Mont Blanc and the Matterhorn in Europe, and El Capitan in the USA (a 900-metre-high slab of granite!). She has hand-cycled the length of Japan and through mountain ranges in Asia. She's even taken to the water and sea kayaked along the coast of Canada and around Corsica in the Mediterranean.

CROSSING GREENLAND

One particularly tough challenge was crossing 700 kilometres (over 430 miles) of the Greenland Ice Cap in 2007. She used a special 'sit-ski' which she adapted using rope, duct tape and a plastic sledge, pulling herself across the ice and snow using regular ski poles.

Along with a small team of friends from Finland, she travelled for up to 10 hours a day, skiing for 55 minutes and then resting for 5 before moving on. They needed to cover around 20 kilometres (12 miles) per day, to ensure they'd have enough food to last the trip. At all times, a loud alarm was kept handy to frighten away any polar bears that got too close.

Darke found the sit-ski scary at first because, unlike a bike, it had no steering or brakes. Her paralysis made it hard to control her body temperature, so she hooked up a fish tank thermometer to her feet, to monitor how cold they were getting! The team battled the freezing conditions – around -30°C, generally – as best they could, with hot-water bottles, hot drinks and fatty foods. Darke would wake every morning to find the tendons in her hands locked tight from the previous day's efforts, and would have to gradually work them loose again.

The journey took about a month, travelling east to west. Their route was a straight line across snow-white wilderness, with just one detour: skirting around DYE-2, an abandoned US radar station left over from the Cold War.

Karen Darke was made an MBE in the 2017 New Year Honours for services to sport. She was once asked what she'd tell her younger self if she had the chance, and her answer was a simple one:

'Believe … Never, ever, give up.'

Karen Darke crosses Greenland on her sit-ski.

FERDINAND MAGELLAN
JUAN ELCANO

CIRCUMNAVIGATORS

Under the command of Portuguese navigator Ferdinand Magellan, five ships carrying a crew of over 270 men set out from Seville, Spain, in 1519. Three years later, only one ship returned with just nineteen survivors, but in that time they had completed the first voyage around the world in human history.

SETTING SAIL WEST

The purpose of the expedition was to find a trade route to eastern Asia by going west through the Americas. Christopher Columbus had attempted the same thing about thirty years earlier, but stopped at South America. Weeks after they set sail, Magellan's fleet sighted Brazil and anchored close to Rio before following the coast south. The weather had turned and was getting steadily worse. Supplies were already running short and on top of that, the mainly Spanish crew didn't like having a Portuguese captain and weren't convinced that a route around South America even existed. Tempers flared, fights broke out and in early 1520 there was a violent mutiny.

Magellan quickly put a stop to it. He couldn't punish all those involved – including a Spanish naval officer called Juan Elcano – because he'd be short of crewmen. He had the ringleaders executed and their bodies put ashore while others, Elcano included, were kept in chains for many days.

There was an uneasy peace aboard Magellan's ships, but it didn't last long. Less than a month later, one of the ships was wrecked. The crew were all rescued, which meant that space aboard the remaining vessels became very cramped. Just days before the expedition rounded the southern tip of South America – what would become known as the Straits of Magellan – there was another mutiny and one of the ships turned back and headed home.

CALMER WATERS

After the rough South Atlantic seas, these new waters seemed calm, which is why Magellan named them the Pacific Ocean. He estimated that the Pacific would take a week or so to cross. It took three months. The crew were reduced to eating rats and sawdust to survive and scurvy plagued almost every member of the crew.

At long last, down to roughly 150 men, they reached the island of Guam and then sailed on to the Philippines. Here, they met *further* trouble! Magellan befriended a local leader and got involved in a battle with a rival tribe. Another forty crewmen were killed in the fight, Magellan among them. Elcano, who had taken part in the first mutiny, then took control of the expedition.

They finally had some good luck when they reached the Spice Islands and traded goods for an extremely valuable cargo of cloves and cinnamon. However, a leaky hull forced one of the two remaining ships to turn back, still fully manned as there was now no room for the crew on the final (and smallest) vessel. The damaged ship didn't make it.

Elcano's ship, the *Victoria,* headed across the Indian Ocean and around the Cape of Good Hope at the southernmost point of Africa, making for Spain as fast as it could. There were more deaths from starvation, with rations soon reduced to a few grains of rice per day. In September 1522, the survivors limped back home. They'd travelled a total of 67,500 kilometres (42,000 miles) almost by accident, since none of them had set out to circumnavigate the globe.

The *Victoria* battles the elements on a round-the-world trip.

AMELIA EARHART
AMY JOHNSON
BESSIE COLEMAN

AVIATORS

Amelia Earhart, Amy Johnson and Bessie Coleman were early aviators who between them broke barriers as well as records. All three have inspired generations but had their careers cut short by tragic accidents.

AMELIA EARHART
1897—1937

AMELIA EARHART

From an early age, Earhart was a bit of a daredevil. She would climb trees, whizz down hills on a sled and hunt rats with an air rifle! Her daredevil streak didn't disappear as an adult and in 1920, at an air show in California, USA, her life changed forever. She went for a ten-minute ride in a small plane and from that moment on she knew she simply had to fly. She cut her hair short and bought a leather jacket, so she'd look like other female pilots of the time.

In 1928, she became the first woman to make a flight across the Atlantic Ocean as part of a three-person crew, but she itched to be the first woman to do the trip alone. Four years later she achieved that goal, marking the start of many flying firsts, which included ...

- 1932 - first person to fly the Atlantic twice
- 1933 - first woman to fly non-stop all the way across the USA
- 1935 - first person to fly solo from Hawaii (in the middle of the Pacific) to California
- 1935 - first person to fly solo non-stop from Mexico to New York

To keep herself in the air, she raised money through sponsorship, writing, lecture tours and what we'd now call 'celebrity branding' – you could buy Amelia Earhart clothes and pack them in your Amelia Earhart luggage!

Amelia Earhart flies in her signature red plane.

FLYING AROUND THE WORLD

In 1937, she took off from California with her navigator, Fred Noonan. Travelling eastward, she aimed to be the first pilot to fly around the world. After about four weeks, they'd completed 35,000 kilometres (22,000 miles) of the journey. Everything was going well.

The final 11,000 kilometres (7,000 miles) would be over the Pacific Ocean. They took off from New Guinea on 2nd July, heading northeast. They stayed in radio contact for a while, but then ... nothing. The aircraft simply vanished.

For decades, their disappearance was a total mystery. Many theories were suggested over the years but the most likely explanation is that their aircraft ditched into waters close to the remote Pacific island Nikumaroro. Human remains were found on the island in 1940, but it wasn't until studies were done in 2017 that they were thought to be Earhart's. What exactly happened is still unknown.

AMY JOHNSON

On the other side of the Atlantic, English aviator Amy Johnson was setting flying records of her own. In 1930, she became the first woman to fly solo from the UK to Australia. Piloting a second-hand 'Gipsy Moth' biplane called *Jason*, she travelled 18,000 kilometres (11,000 miles) in 19 days. This was all the more remarkable because she'd only been flying as a hobby for less than a year. Just like Earhart, Johnson had a string of aviation successes, including ...

- 1931 - she and co-pilot Jack Humphreys were the first to fly from London to Moscow, Russia, in one day. They carried on to the Far East and set a record time for flying from the UK to Japan.
- 1932 - she snatched the speed record for flying from Britain to South Africa from a flyer called Jim Mollison, whom she'd just married! Her time was later beaten, but she regained the record in 1936.
- 1934 - Johnson and Mollison were forced to pull out of an air race to Australia, but not before they'd set another speed record, this time for a flight from Britain to India.

During World War II, Johnson became a first officer in the Air Transport Auxiliary. However, in January 1941, bad weather forced her off course while piloting a training plane from Blackpool to Oxford. Over Herne Bay, near the mouth of the River Thames, her aircraft nose-dived and she was seen parachuting to safety. She landed in the river and brave efforts were made to rescue her, but currents were too strong and the water was icy cold. Her body was never recovered.

In 2016, to mark the 75th anniversary of Amy Johnson's death, statues of her were unveiled in Herne Bay and near her childhood home in Hull.

Amy Johnson touches down in Australia.

Bessie Coleman takes to the skies to perform spectacular stunts.

BESSIE COLEMAN

Earhart and Johnson, for all their skill and courage, tended to fly in straight lines. Bessie Coleman from Texas, USA, was an expert at what was called 'barnstorming'. This type of flying meant performing all kinds of jaw-dropping, death-defying aerial stunts. Barnstormers, sometimes called flying circuses, were hugely popular in the USA in the 1920s.

Coleman grew up determined to make a success of her life. As an avid reader, she found inspiration in accounts of the flying 'aces' (military pilots) of World War I. Her brothers had both served in the war and teased her about her chances of becoming an aviator, which made her even more determined than ever.

Coleman's heritage was both African American and Native American. She quickly discovered that no flying school in the country would teach either women or people of colour. But this didn't stop her – she simply learned French and set sail for Europe to enrol in flying school in Paris!

QUEEN BESS

Ten months later, pilot's licence in hand, Coleman returned to the USA and quickly became a sensational barnstormer. Her aerobatic stunts and tricks – figure-of-eights, loop-the-loops, swooping dives and even landings with the engine turned off – had the press calling her 'Queen Bess'. At all times, she aimed to be a positive role model for women and for people of colour, refusing to perform at shows where crowds were split up according to skin colour.

Like Earhart and Johnson, her career ended suddenly. In April 1926, she took a test flight in an aircraft she'd recently saved up to buy. Her mechanic was at the controls and she left her seatbelt off so that she could lean out to check various things while in the air. The biplane broke down and Coleman was thrown out of it before it hit the ground. She died instantly.

Bessie Coleman was a fearless pioneer, and not only in the air. Her dream of a flying school for African Americans became a reality in 1929 when the Bessie Coleman Aero Club was set up in Los Angeles.

SURESH BISWAS

ADVENTURER

Suresh Biswas was a restless kid. He was born in Bengal, in the east of India, and spent most of his childhood either playing what we'd now call extreme sports or else finding reckless and dangerous things to do!

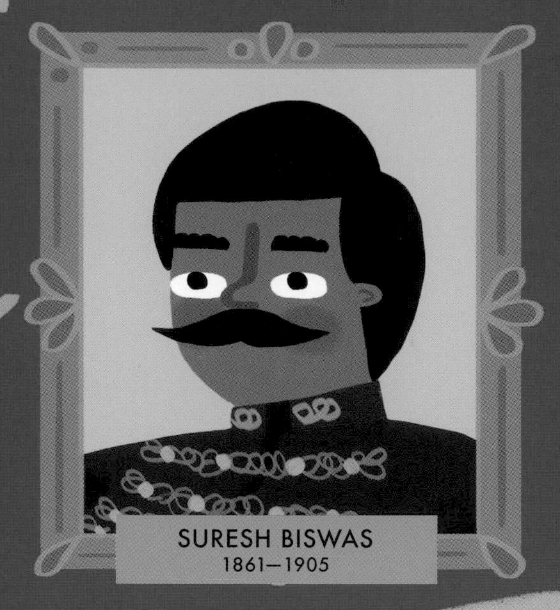

At the age of fourteen he ran away from home and stowed away on a ship bound for Rangoon (now known as Yangon) in Burma (now Myanmar). This was the start of many years spent travelling, adventuring and generally living life in as swashbuckling a way as possible. However, Biswas realised that there wasn't much to interest him in Rangoon so – pausing only to rescue a young woman from a burning building – he hopped on a steamship to London.

JOINING THE CIRCUS

For a while, he scratched a living in the slums of the East End. On a visit to Kent, he got talking to some circus people and their stories about the perils and pitfalls of circus life sparked his imagination. This was just the kind of hazardous lifestyle that would suit him!

The following day, he offered his services as a weightlifter and acrobat. The ringmaster took one look at this scrawny seventeen-year-old and said he could have a job if he could beat their best wrestler in a fight ... and he did! Biswas joined the circus and became a lion tamer.

ADVENTURES IN BRAZIL

Some years later Biswas continued his travels and went to Brazil. He loved the country and decided to settle there. For a while he worked for the Brazilian royal family as a keeper in their private zoo but soon joined the army, where he did well and was promoted to captain.

In 1894, the Brazilian navy staged a violent uprising. They launched an attack on the city of Niterói, but troops under Biswas's command kept them at bay and played a major part in putting a stop to the whole rebellion. His heroism made him an instant national hero and he became a respected and popular figure in the poshest social circles of the capital city, Rio de Janeiro.

Suresh Biswas is celebrated as a hero in Rio de Janeiro.

History hasn't been kind to Suresh Biswas – records of his adventures are few and far between, and most of the last twenty years of his life left no evidence at all. Oddly, he's frequently referred to as 'Colonel Suresh Biswas' but he was never a colonel – his army rank was captain. Even so, from what we can piece together, he must have lived one of the most unusual lives of the 1800s.

Freya Stark meets local people on her travels through the Middle East.

FREYA STARK
DERVLA MURPHY

TRAVEL WRITERS

Writing about your travels, no matter how near or far they take you, is a good way to remember your adventures. It's also a way for others to share your journeys. Two great travel writers who've delighted many readers in this way are Freya Stark and Dervla Murphy.

FREYA STARK

Freya Stark was born in Paris, France, but grew up in Italy. Throughout her life, she travelled to the Middle East and Asia, including Turkey, Iran, Syria, Lebanon, Iraq and Afghanistan. Wherever she went, usually alone, she spoke the local language and often lived with local people in order to understand their culture. She once said that she never travelled in order to write, only to explore.

FREYA STARK
1893–1993

She was intelligent and forthright, but above all fearless. In the early 1930s, she made trips into Luristan, a remote part of Iran where few Westerners had ever been, encountering dangerous and lawless tribes in the 'Valley of the Assassins'. In 1941, during World War II, she risked death by smuggling goods into the besieged British Embassy in Baghdad.

Over the years, she wrote more than two dozen travel books, many of which are still regarded as all-time greats.

DERVLA MURPHY

Dervla Murphy was born in Lismore, Ireland, and still lives there to this day. On her tenth birthday, she was given a second-hand bicycle and an atlas. This was the beginning of Murphy's great adventure and it wasn't long before she was determined to cycle all over the world, inspired by Freya Stark's travels!

DERVLA MURPHY
b. 1931

Murphy's first great adventure was in 1963, when she cycled from Dunkirk, on the north coast of France, all the way to Delhi, the capital of India. She wrote about the trip in one of her most famous books, *Full Tilt*.

For over fifty years, she travelled all across the Middle East and Far East, Europe, Africa and South America. Like Stark, she never stayed in hotels but preferred to live alongside the local people so that her writing would reflect the ordinary person's point of view. Murphy completed almost all of her travels by bicycle and she mostly travelled alone (except when her daughter joined her).

SOME TRAVEL TROUBLES

Murphy faced lots of challenges on her travels and she once wrote that disasters are unavoidable on a long trek. She had dysentery in Pakistan, hepatitis in Madagascar, tick bite fever in South Africa, fractured bones in Romania and Siberia – but she took them all in her stride! There were plenty of other misadventures too, the most painful of which, she said, was a triple tooth abscess in Cameroon.

Her life at home reflects the same plain and simple approach she took to her travels: no central heating, no washing machine, no car and definitely no mobile phone or TV. She writes her books by hand, and then tidies them up with an old-fashioned electric typewriter.

Travel writers like Stark and Murphy, and many more besides, can help us understand and appreciate what it's like to see parts of the world we may never get the chance to set foot in ourselves. All kinds of adventures around the globe could be just a couple of chapters away ...

Dervla Murphy cycles across the world.

XU FU

SORCERER AND EXPLORER

There are lots of legends about journeys to mythical places like King Arthur's Camelot or the lost lands of Atlantis and Lemuria. One of the most interesting is the story of Xu Fu, because it's a mixture of historical fact and ancient myth that leaves us with a strange and unsolvable puzzle.

Xu Fu was employed as court sorcerer by the first emperor of China, Qin Shi Huang, who started work on what would eventually become the Great Wall of China. Qin Shi Huang had a constant fear of death and was determined to find an elixir of life – something that would enable him to live forever. He commanded Xu Fu to find it for him, and here's where myth starts to replace fact.

THE QUEST FOR THE ELIXIR OF LIFE

Xu Fu was ordered to travel to the legendary Penglai Mountain and consult the 1,000-year-old wizard Anqi Sheng, someone the emperor claimed to have met on his travels. In 219 BCE, Xu Fu set off as instructed but returned some years later empty-handed. Qin Shi Huang questioned him angrily about the reason for his failure. Xu Fu, probably thinking to himself that he needed a good excuse, said there was a giant sea monster blocking the way to Penglai. 'Fair enough,' said the emperor, 'take archers with you next time to shoot the sea monster. If you come back with nothing again, you die.'

So Xu Fu left again in 210 BCE, this time with sixty ships crewed by 5,000 men and women. None of them ever returned. It's possible they sailed away into the sunset, realising their quest was a pointless one and wanting to avoid execution. However, Japanese legend says that Xu Fu landed in Japan, mistaking Mount Fuji for Penglai, and literally became a god!

Various historical clues support this ...

• Japan's prehistoric Jōmon culture, which had lasted thousands of years and was roughly equivalent to the Stone Age in the West, came to an end around this time. The Yayoi culture (Bronze Age and Iron Age) that followed it was much closer to the culture of China.

• Chinese words and tools started to be used in Japan at that time. The capital city, Nara, ended up closely modelled on Qin Shi Huang's capital, Chang'an. Xu Fu's expedition would certainly have brought many Chinese ideas with it.

• Legend says that Xu Fu was worshipped as 'Jofuku', God of Farming and Medicine, because he improved the quality of life in Japan with new methods of growing crops, as well as plants that could be used for medicine. Temples dedicated to Jofuku can be found in Japan to this day.

It's even been suggested that Xu Fu and the legendary first emperor of Japan, Jimmu, were the same person. This is unlikely, but nobody can be sure one way or the other – reliable records weren't kept in Japan until around the sixth century CE. Whether or not Xu Fu became a great ruler, his ships could well have been the first to reach Japan from China, and so began a connection that would last for centuries.

Xu Fu searches for the legendary Elixir of Life.

ANNIE KOPCHOVSKY

CYCLIST

It started with a bet. The story goes that two wealthy businessmen in Boston, USA, argued whether a woman would be capable of riding a bike around the world in fifteen months or less, *while also* supporting herself by earning $5,000 (about $125,000 today) during the trip.

ANNIE KOPCHOVSKY
1870–1947

Annie Kopchovsky, originally from Latvia, took up the challenge. In the 1890s, bicycles were becoming a popular everyday transport for the first time. The journey was bound to attract attention and Kopchovsky was very good at being noticed. She planned to raise the $5,000 partly by giving talks about her travels along the way but mostly by advertising. Just as sports teams today sell space on their kit, so Kopchovsky sold ad space on her bike, her clothes and even her *name*. On the day she left Boston, in June 1894, she arranged for the Londonderry Lithia Spring Water Company to present her with her first $100 in front of the crowd who'd gathered to see her off. In return, she hung an ad on her bike and called herself Annie Londonderry for the rest of the trip! Throughout her journey, she also sold signed photos and souvenir badges.

READY TO GO

She set off carrying only a change of clothes and a pearl-handled pistol. Astonishingly, she'd *never ridden* a bike until a couple of days earlier. Kopchovsky attracted headlines, praise and scandal in equal measure – all because she was a woman travelling alone.

At first, she headed west across America and nearly gave up. Progress was far too slow, so she swapped her bike for a much lighter one and swapped her skirts for trousers that were easier to cycle in. At Chicago, with four of her fifteen months already used up, she turned around and started again, heading east this time.

Whenever she encountered an ocean, she took a steamship (this wasn't cheating, there was no rule forbidding it). She rode down through France, across North Africa and into the Middle East. In those days, there were very few proper road systems anywhere in the world. Most of the time, Kopchovsky bumped along rough tracks and rode beside railway lines, where the ground was flatter.

BUMPS ALONG THE JOURNEY

Kopchovsky crashed and was robbed along her journey but because she was on her own, without any backup at all, she simply had to grit her teeth and carry on. If she punctured a tyre, she picked up her bike and walked to the nearest place she could get it repaired. Travelling alone meant that she had to collect signatures from American diplomats stationed in various cities along the route, to prove she'd been there. She arrived back in Boston with just a few days to spare, nursing a broken wrist from a recent fall.

Kopchovsky was so keen to drum up headlines that the talks she gave during her trip, and her written accounts of it afterwards, were filled with dramatic 'improvements'. She'd chased tigers in India! She'd been a prisoner in Japan! She was a poor orphan, a medical student, the inventor of a new method of handwriting! None of it was true. Was there even a bet? We'll never know. Kopchovsky played down her real achievement: a trip that even today would be a severe test of physical and mental strength for anyone.

Annie Kopchovsky sets out on her mission to cycle around the world.

ERIK THE RED LEIF ERIKSSON

NORSE EXPLORERS

In the days of the Vikings, history was recorded in the form of 'sagas' – epic tales of mighty heroes. It's mostly thanks to these sagas that we know about Erik Thorvaldsson and his son Leif Eriksson, who each made long journeys to uncharted lands.

THE SAGA OF ERIK THE RED

Erik Thorvaldsson was known as 'Erik the Red' because of the colour of his hair and beard, although it might as well have been for the colour of his sword – he seemed to make a habit of killing people!

In 982, while banished from Iceland for three years (for, guess what, killing someone) he set sail and headed west across the stormy waters of the north Atlantic. He'd heard stories about a mysterious land, spotted from the sea 100 years earlier by a sailor named Gunnbjörn Ulfsson. Determined to find this land, he kept going in roughly the same direction for 1,700 kilometres (1,000 miles) until he landed at the southern tip of a massive island.

ERIK THE RED
c. 950—c. 1003

After exploring this island for a while, he decided to set up a permanent colony there. He returned to Iceland and told people what he'd discovered, encouraging them to return with him by calling the place Greenland (which sounded a lot nicer than a more accurate name, like Freezing-Snow-and-Rock-Covered-Land).

In 985, twenty five ships set off to the new colony at Greenland to start a new life. Only fourteen arrived but two small settlements were established which lasted for hundreds of years. Erik the Red lived the rest of his days there with his wife and four children, including the son who'd go one better than his dad in the exploring business ...

THE SAGA OF LEIF ERIKSSON

Leif's nickname was Leif the Lucky. Like his father, he'd heard tales of an unknown land far to the west – even further away than Greenland – tales this time told by a trader called Bjarni Herjólfsson.

With the curiosity and determination he'd inherited from his father, Leif and a crew of about twenty-five set off in 999 (or possibly 1000, we can't be sure) to look for this uncharted place. He invited his dad to go along with him, but on his way to the ship Erik fell off his horse. He took this as a bad omen and refused to go!

According to one saga, Leif reached his goal only because his ship was blown off course (which may explain where he got that 'Lucky' nickname). The ship docked at a couple of places along the coast of this strange new land, before stopping further south. Leif and his men discovered rich forests and grapevines, and so Leif named his new discovery Vinland.

Leif had actually landed on the continent of North America, 500 years before Christopher Columbus arrived, believing himself to be the first European to get there. We don't know exactly where Leif's Vinland was located, but remains of a Viking settlement were discovered in 1963, in what is now Newfoundland in Canada.

Unlike Erik in Greenland, Leif never established a permanent colony in Vinland. That may be why his voyage of discovery remained in the background of history for so long, while Columbus got all the attention!

Leif Eriksson and his
crew discover rich
forests in a new land.

BARBARA HILLARY

POLAR EXPLORER

One sure sign of a born explorer is this: tell them something's never been done before and they'll want to make it the very next thing they do. And that is exactly what Barbara Hillary did!

Hillary had a long career as a nurse in New York, USA, and after she retired she took a trip to Canada, where she spent her time photographing polar bears. This trip sparked her interest in the icy north and Hillary now had a new goal ...

A CHANCE TO BE THE FIRST

The first woman to reach the North Pole was Ann Bancroft, a teacher from Minnesota, USA. However, the moment Barbara Hillary discovered that no African American woman had ever been there, she knew that this was what she wanted to do.

Training for an Arctic expedition wasn't easy in a busy and chaotic city. She'd never even been on skis before, let alone driven a snowmobile or a pack of dogs. Not to be put off, she trained for her great adventure by pulling a plastic sled along a beach, with a big bag of sand on top of it. The fact that she was seventy-six years old made no difference to her determination to succeed.

Barbara Hillary celebrates as she reaches the North Pole.

REACHING THE NORTH POLE

On 23rd April 2007, it was time to put all of her training to the test. Hillary was dropped off by helicopter, along with two guides, on the ice floe at the temporary Russian base Camp Barneo, roughly 100 kilometres (60 miles) from the North Pole. Arctic travel is dangerous and Hillary risked the intense cold, sudden shifts in the weather and movement in the ice underfoot to complete her goal.

Hillary was determined. After a long trek across the ice, wrapped in layers of long underwear and a bulky red and black snowsuit, she finally reached the North Pole. She was so delighted that she jumped up and down with joy! Forgetting the cold for a moment, she pulled off her gloves to do a thumbs-up for a photo – instant frozen hand! She got frostbite in her thumb and learned never to do that again.

THE ADVENTURE CONTINUES

Hillary's adventures didn't end there. On 6th January 2011, at the age of seventy-nine, she became the first African American woman to reach the South Pole too! After her polar voyages, Barbara Hillary became an internationally known public speaker, inspiring others with her incredible determination and adventurous excursions. She also started planning her *next* trip ...

There's one more reason why her story is so remarkable: some years before she went to the North Pole, she'd had surgery to remove part of a lung – she'd survived cancer, twice. She not only completed two very challenging journeys in her seventies, she did it with a reduced capacity to breathe!

SIDNEY REILLY

SPY

He was nicknamed the 'Ace of Spies'. Nobody can be certain where he came from and he adopted many aliases throughout his life, but his original name was *probably* Sigmund (or maybe Georgi) Rosenblum and he was *probably* Russian (but he said he was Irish).

Reilly was, by all accounts, a charming and well-dressed man who spoke seven languages fluently and was a master of disguise. He was also ruthless, double-crossing and greedy, making money out of trading in weapons and other goods during wartime. The writer Ian Fleming even used him as an inspiration for his fictional spy James Bond!

From 1899, he had a British passport in the name of Sidney Reilly (although he was never a British citizen) and it was under this name that he worked for the Secret Intelligence Service. For twenty years, Reilly was involved in an astonishing series of undercover operations, plots, counter-plots and conspiracies. It's hard to pick facts out of the clouds of mystery which surround him, but it's been claimed that among his daring exploits were ...

THE GERMAN WEAPONS PLOT

In 1909, Britain wanted to know how prepared Germany was for a war. Reilly went undercover as a welder at the Krupp weapons factory in Essen. The plans and blueprints he was after were locked away in an office to which he had no access. So he volunteered to be in the factory's fire brigade, which meant he could be there at night. In the early hours, he picked the lock on the office door, stole the plans and was halfway back to England before the theft was discovered.

THE WORLD WAR I PLOT

Dropped behind German lines by parachute, Reilly maintained his cover by joining the German army! He seized an unexpected opportunity and put on the uniform of a high-ranking officer who'd been killed. Disguised in this way, he attended a meeting of the German High Command. He took notes on all the military secrets that were discussed and immediately sent them back to London.

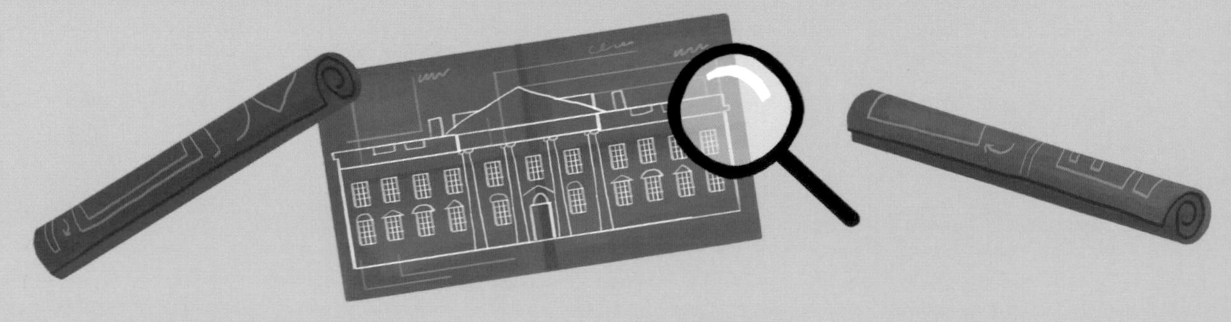

THE RUSSIAN REVOLUTION PLOT

When Russia dropped out of World War I, Reilly became part of a team whose mission was to overthrow the new communist government. Reilly planned to assassinate Lenin, the communists' leader, but the plot was discovered at the last minute. Most of the agents involved were caught and killed. With the Russian secret service swarming through Moscow, Reilly narrowly escaped the city by posing as a secretary with the German Embassy.

His list of adventures is enormous: spying for the Japanese, joining the Royal Flying Corps in Canada, saving British diplomats in Brazil. But how many are true is a matter of debate. Reilly was an elusive and shady man, whose only real loyalty was to himself. Nobody could quite trust him, which is why he was finally sacked from the British secret service in 1921!

Sidney Reilly: a true master of disguise.

MARY FIELDS

STAGECOACH DRIVER

Life in the frontier lands of the USA in the 1800s was often harsh, squalid and lawless. To live there, you had to be tough and none came tougher than Mary Fields. Born a slave and only freed in 1865 after the American Civil War, she became such a legend that it's hard to be sure what's fact and what's fiction about her life.

MARY FIELDS
c. 1832–1914

In 1885, she arrived at the settlement in Cascade, Montana, to work at a Christian mission and school run by nuns for Native American girls. She chopped wood, carried out repairs, built the schoolhouse, did the laundry, looked after the chickens and tended the garden. Anyone who walked on the lawn after she'd just cut it did so at their peril! Fields was a tall and imposing woman, with the temperament of a grizzly bear – tough talking and strong enough to knock a man over with one blow when she was in her seventies!

FACING DANGER

Field's steely nerves were tested one night as she made her way through the rocky wilderness to collect provisions for the mission. Completely alone and miles from help, Fields and her wagon were attacked by a pack of hungry wolves. Her horses panicked, knocking the wagon over and running off into the night. She was left alone in the dark, with only a small lamp to help her see. Keeping her back to the upturned cart, so the wolves couldn't sneak up behind her, she spent the entire night using her shotgun to fend off one attack after another.

Other people might have been rattled by this experience and hurried home to find help. But not Fields. When it was light, she heaved the wagon upright, tracked down the remaining horses and delivered the provisions to the nuns. The only thing broken was a tub of molasses, which the bishop in charge of the mission made her pay for with her own money.

WORKING FOR THE US POSTAL SERVICE

At the age of sixty, Fields became the first African American, and only the second woman, to join the US Postal Service. Here she earned the nickname Stagecoach Mary and for eight years she delivered mail all over central Montana, taking her wagon (and her mule, Moses) through some of the most dangerous territory in the country. Hostile Native Americans, murderous outlaws, extreme weather, deadly wild animals – you name it, she braved it. Through blizzards, baking heat or driving rain, she never once failed to make her deliveries on time. When snow got too thick for her horses, she slung her bag on her back and made it through on foot.

She retired in 1901, but still ran her own laundry business. It's easy to get the impression that she was a harsh person, but she had a softer side too: she was kind and compassionate, liked growing flowers and was a much-in-demand babysitter in later life. She was so loved in Cascade that they had an annual school holiday on her birthday.

Mary Fields was brave and fiercely independent in a hostile place and at a time when women and people of colour were expected to do as they were told.

She most certainly did not.

Mary Fields drives her stagecoach through the rocky wilderness.

GEORGE SCHUSTER

ENGINEER AND DRIVER

The early years of motoring were full of experiments and oddities. The 'Great Race' of 1908, set up by France's *Le Matin* and America's *New York Times* newspapers, was designed to test the limits of automobile technology and prove that the motor car was truly the transport of the future.

The racers: one from Germany, a car made by the Protos company; one from Italy, a Zust; one from the USA, a Thomas Flyer; three from France, a Sizaire-Naudin, a De Dion and a Moto-Bloc.

Assorted mechanics and hangers-on piled into the cars alongside the designated drivers. All six cars had open tops and most didn't have windscreens. Beside the driver in the Thomas Flyer was a *New York Times* reporter and George Schuster, a mechanic who'd only been recruited twelve hours earlier and had no idea what he'd let himself in for.

The route: west from New York across the USA, north to Alaska, over the frozen-solid waters of the Bering Strait then down through Russia and right across Europe to Paris!

AT THE STARTING LINE

On a freezing cold day in February, in front of a crowd of 250,000 people, the starting gun fired in New York's Times Square, signalling the beginning of an epic adventure! The race took place in winter to ensure that the Bering Strait would be solidly iced over. However, it also meant that crossing the USA would be extremely difficult, with deep snow and equally deep mud for long distances. Only nine cars had ever driven across the country before, all of them during summer!

George Schuster zooms across the globe in a Thomas Flyer.

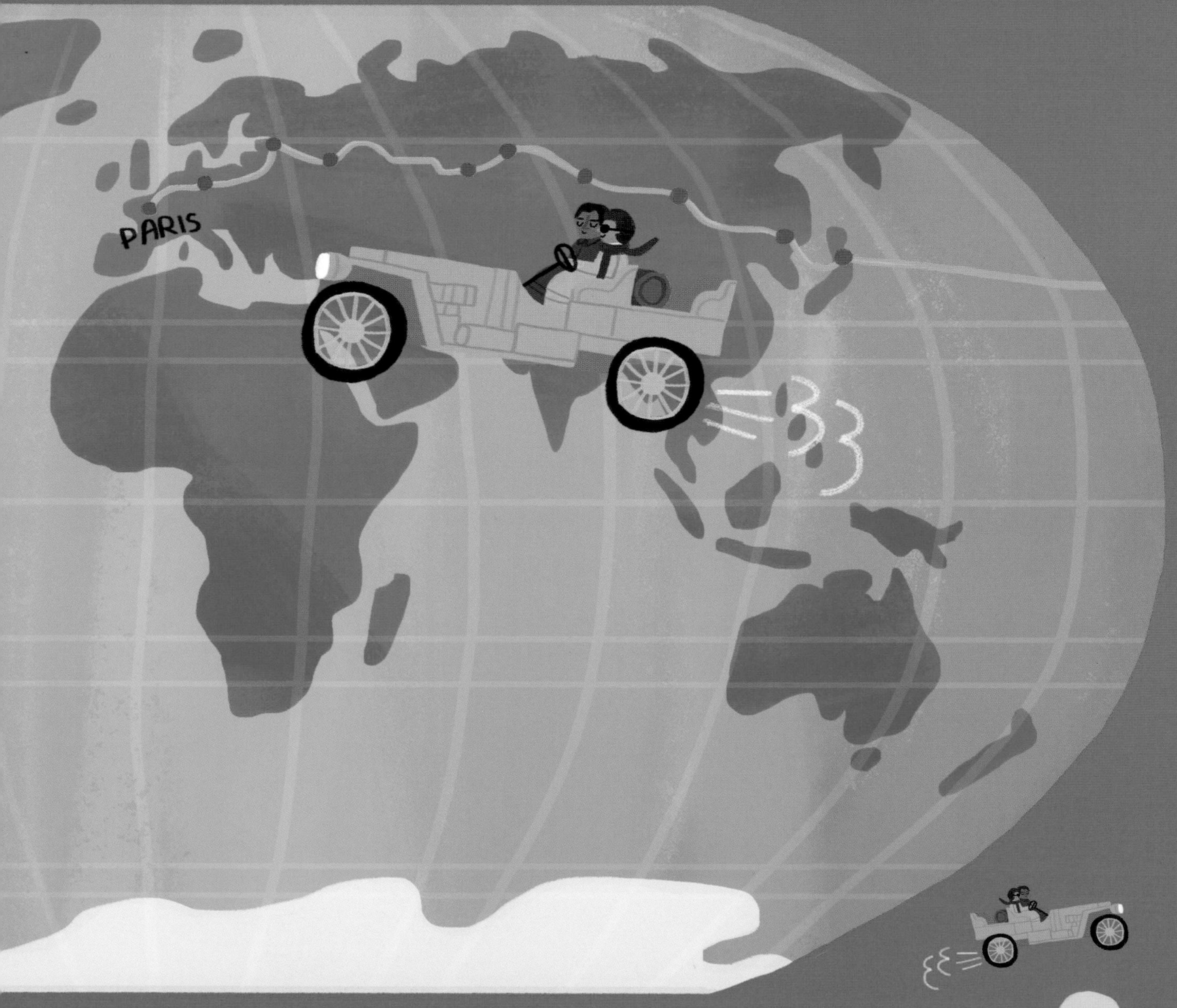

THE RACE CONTINUES

As the racers soon discovered, the world still didn't have many actual roads. These clunky, delicate automobiles bumped along on rocky, slippery, dusty or boggy surfaces that even a modern car would find hard-going!

The Sizaire-Naudin broke down after less than 160 kilometres (100 miles). One down, five to go.

All the competitors started the race in a friendly spirit of sportsmanship and international co-operation. However, this didn't last long. The teams quickly realised that just a little extra effort here or there could make all the difference. They settled into a routine of getting up at 5.00 a.m., driving until 8.00 p.m., letting the mechanics do repairs overnight and never, ever, lending the other teams spare parts or fuel.

The Zust, the De Dion and the Thomas Flyer took the lead, with the Protos and the Moto-Bloc some way behind. The Moto-Bloc hit mechanical trouble and dropped out. Two down, four to go.

The Thomas Flyer reached San Francisco, on the west coast of the USA, way ahead of the others. By this point, the team's mechanic, George Schuster, had taken the wheel when the original driver left to take part in another race! The car headed north until the heavy ice and snow of Alaska blocked the way. The race organisers decided to scrap the Bering Strait idea and take the cars across the Pacific by boat instead, first to Japan, then on to Russia. By the time the Flyer turned back from Alaska, it had gone from first place to last ...

When the cars reached Russia, the teams found driving conditions were even worse: the warmer spring weather had turned the ground into a marshy paste. Fuel was harder to find because there were fewer vehicles in that part of the world. Schuster and the Flyer edged ahead again, but lost a whole day trapped in mud, and Schuster, who spoke no Russian, kept getting lost.

Finally, the lack of petrol forced the De Dion out of the race. Three down, three to go.

THE FINAL STRETCH

Crossing Europe, the Protos gained a three-day lead on the Flyer, who was ahead of the Zust. All seemed lost for Schuster when the Protos arrived in Paris on 26th July 1908. However, the organisers gave the Protos a fifteen-day penalty – back in the USA, they'd briefly used a train to move their car!

The Flyer still had a chance! But they ran into trouble again when they got to Paris. The car was stopped by a policeman for having a broken headlight. The Flyer was only allowed to carry on when Schuster borrowed a passing bicycle with a light and strapped it to the side of the car. The Flyer finally crossed the finish line at 6.00 p.m. on 30th July, winning the race.

What happened to the Zust? It eventually turned up in September!

George Schuster navigates the way through muddy conditions in Russia.

HARRIET TUBMAN

ACTIVIST

MARY BOWSER

SPY

The American Civil War of 1861–1865 was fought for several reasons, but mainly over slavery. The country's northern states wanted to abolish it, but the southern states didn't. Among many heroic stories from that time are those of two women born into slavery who fought for its abolition.

HARRIET TUBMAN

By the time the Civil War broke out, Harriet Tubman was already highly skilled at undercover missions to free slaves from captivity. In 1849, she had escaped to Pennsylvania, where slavery had already been abolished, by walking 145 kilometres (90 miles) north from the plantation (a large farm growing crops) where she lived. Determined to free others, she spent the 1850s working for the Underground Railroad, a secret network of anti-slavery supporters and safe places where escapees could hide.

Tubman made many trips back into slave-owning territory and helped over 300 people to safety, including members of her own family. When travelling in public, she would disguise herself and her runaways to look like they were busy running errands. This saved her life at least twice, when she accidentally encountered men who'd previously 'owned' her. The first time, she shook some chickens she was carrying – their squawking allowed her to keep her head down, as if shushing them, and so avoid the man's gaze. The second time, she was on a train – as the man walked towards her she calmly picked up a newspaper and pretended to read it until the danger had passed.

Harriet Tubman travels in disguise as she leads slaves to freedom.

Although her bravery would raise the spirits of escapees, she wouldn't hesitate to browbeat anyone who wanted to turn back or give themselves up. Punishments for escapees, and those helping them, were severe. Rewards were offered for the capture of runaways and Tubman herself had a price on her head. She risked being caught by slave-catchers or their dogs almost daily.

Tubman's experience with the Underground Railroad made her valuable as a spy too: in 1863, she guided soldiers to three plantations in South Carolina. Over 750 slaves were rescued in the raid!

Mary Bowser spies on Confederate leader Jefferson Davis.

MARY BOWSER

Mary Bowser worked as a spy for the Union (anti-slavery) forces during the Civil War. She was a freed slave who was part of an undercover group run by Elizabeth Van Lew, the daughter of a wealthy family in Richmond, Virginia, a place in the USA that was part of the (pro-slavery) Confederacy.

To Unionists, Abraham Lincoln was US president, but according to Confederates, it was Jefferson Davis in Richmond. With Van Lew's help, Bowser began working at functions run by Varina Davis, who was married to Jefferson Davis. Bowser was very good at acting and pretended to be a slow-witted slave called 'Ellen Bond' (there's a good name for a spy!). Soon 'Miss Bond' was working at Davis's home. Cleaning or waiting at tables, Bowser heard all kinds of secret presidential conversations about the war. Disguised as a slave, she went almost unnoticed.

It was illegal to teach slaves to read, so Davis thought nothing of leaving important papers lying around. Bowser kept her literacy secret and was able to sift through documents. She had an excellent memory and could pass information to the Unionists word for word. Eventually, Davis realised there was a spy around and tied himself in knots trying to find out who it was! Even then, Bowser remained undetected for a while but finally had to make a run for it shortly before the war ended.

What happened to her after that? We don't know for sure. Perhaps silently fading from the pages of history is what a spy prefers ...

SIR RANULPH FIENNES

WRITER AND EXPLORER

It would be hard to find anyone anywhere who fits the word 'adventurer' better than Ranulph Twisleton-Wykeham-Fiennes. Since leaving military service in 1970, his list of exploits as explorer, climber and athlete has been extraordinary, including ...

SIR RANULPH FIENNES
b. 1944

THE TRANSGLOBE EXPEDITION

In 1979, after nearly eight years of careful planning, Fiennes and two army friends set off from London to (roughly) follow the Greenwich Meridian (where the eastern and western hemispheres meet) all the way around the world: south via Africa to Antarctica, then north across the Pacific Ocean, Alaska and the Arctic and back to London – all done by surface travel (although aircraft were part of their large support team which organised supplies and equipment).

They crossed the Sahara Desert in temperatures of over 36°C, then travelled though the swamps and jungles of Mali and the Ivory Coast. They were the first to trek across Antarctica in a straight line, driving snowmobiles through uncharted regions where a sudden fall into a crevasse was a constant danger. At the South Pole, they stopped long enough to play a game of cricket.

On the way back, Fiennes and one of his co-travellers got stuck on a drifting sheet of ice for over three months before being picked up by their supply vessel, the *Benjamin Bowring*. The whole trip took nearly three years, covering a distance of nearly 161,000 kilometres (100,000 miles), and has never been repeated by anyone else. Fiennes's dog, Bothie, did parts of the journey too, travelling by helicopter to become the first dog to visit both poles!

MORE ARCTIC AND ANTARCTIC VOYAGES

Fiennes returned several times to the Arctic and Antarctica, making attempts with fellow adventurer Mike Stroud to walk to the poles unaided, without communication equipment and carrying all his supplies with him. He and Stroud made the longest unsupported polar journey in history in 1992–93 by crossing the Antarctic continent in ninety-three days.

In 2000, he was forced to abandon his solo bid to reach the North Pole, when his sled fell through the ice. In trying to pull it out, he suffered severe frostbite in his hands. His left hand was so bad that, on his return, he was told that in a few months the tips of his fingers and thumb would have to be cut off. Fed up with the pain, he simply did the job himself!

7X7X7

In 2003, again accompanied by Stroud, he became the first person to complete a 7x7x7, running seven marathons on seven consecutive days on seven different continents. As if that wasn't enough, he did it a matter of weeks after having a massive heart attack, which left him in a three-day coma and needing double bypass heart surgery!

There are lots of other examples of his adventurerous spirit, including his 2009 climb up Mount Everest at the age of sixty-five and running a 156-kilometre (97-mile) ultra-marathon across the Sahara. Over the years, his expeditions have raised millions for charities, including Marie Curie Cancer Care and the British Heart Foundation.

Ranulph Fiennes and his dog, Bothie, reach the North Pole.

ISABELLA BIRD

PHOTOGRAPHER AND EXPLORER

Isabella Bird went to a *lot* of places during her lifetime – the USA, Australia, Canada, Japan, Vietnam, India, Hawaii, Malaya, Turkey, North Africa, the Middle East ... and many others! Her accounts of her travels, such as *A Lady's Life in the Rocky Mountains* (about Colorado, USA) and *Six Months in the Sandwich Islands* (about Hawaii) made her well known and respected.

DOCTOR'S ORDERS

From her early childhood in England, Bird suffered from poor health. She had constant problems with her back and was never free of insomnia (an inability to sleep). In 1854, when a doctor told her that sea air would do her good (Victorian doctors often said this when they had no idea how to treat an ailment), her father gave her £100 and told her to take off in whatever direction she wished. This was the beginning of her lifelong passion for adventure.

Like some other dedicated travellers, she preferred to live among the local people wherever she went. She was always restless back home: her itchy feet and fierce independence quickly got her travelling again, often alone, no matter what dangers or discomforts she might face along the way.

At the age of sixty, she gained a new hobby – photography. She was very good at it, and the photographs she took were one of the reasons why her three-year journey to the Far East was perhaps her most important and memorable.

TRAVELS IN CHINA AND BEYOND

Setting off from Liverpool, England, Bird had no idea that she was heading straight into a war. She arrived in Korea just as China and Japan were about to start fighting over it. Within weeks, she was deported and ended up in northern China without any money, with most of her luggage gone, staying in a missionary hospital suffering from malaria and a broken arm. Despite everything, she quickly fell in love with the country and its people and adopted Chinese dress as a courtesy.

Once out of hospital she was off on her adventures again. On a rickety sampan (a flat-bottomed wooden houseboat) with a small crew of hired workmen, she journeyed thousands of kilometres from Shanghai along the length of the Yangtze River, deep into mainland China. The trip was extremely hazardous, with the boat sometimes needing to be dragged up rapids or against powerful currents.

Wherever Isabella Bird went in China, she was stared at simply because locals had never seen a foreigner before. Most of this attention was friendly but some Chinese people believed that Europeans were 'devils'. She had rocks and mud thrown at her several times and, in Sichuan province, she was trapped inside a house by a huge mob who set fire to the building. Bird was rescued at the last minute by a troop of Chinese soldiers.

A PHOTOGRAPHIC RECORD

Throughout her journey, her bulky camera equipment went with her. Overnight, she would often keep her clothes and boots away from the rats and other vermin by hanging them on her camera's chunky wooden tripod. Her pictures were a unique record of ordinary Chinese life at the time, and an important part of her campaigning. She often used her fame to speak out against injustice and, in China's case, she severely criticised Western society for its attitude to Chinese culture. Just as travellers like Mary Kingsley helped change Western attitudes to Africa, so Isabella Bird brought everyday life in China to her readers.

Isabella Bird travels by sampan and photographs her surroundings.

HANNIBAL

ARMY COMMANDER

The Second Punic War was one of the nastiest fights in ancient history ('Punic' means it involved Carthage, which was an empire covering an area that today is part of North Africa and southern Spain). One side was made up of the forces of the Roman Empire, while the other side were the Carthaginians under their leader, Hannibal.

A ROMAN PROBLEM

Hannibal had a problem: he wanted to march his army into Rome, but getting there was close to impossible. If he took his army across the Mediterranean Sea, the Romans' ships would send his men to a watery grave. If he went north from the 'toe' of Italy, he would have to face the Roman legions blocking the way and he'd never get through.

But Hannibal had a solution up his sleeve – a very risky and *very* dangerous one. He would march the entire Carthaginian army, including war elephants and thousands of horses, up the east coast of Spain, into France, across the River Rhône and then up over the Alps (the high mountain range between France and Italy), a journey of around 1,600 kilometres (1,000 miles). Under anyone else's command, normal circumstances, taking men, equipment, supplies and *elephants* over snow-capped peaks would be utterly bonkers, but Hannibal was extremely good at his job.

TREKKING OVER THE ALPS

The route through the mountains was treacherous, and they came under attack from local Gallic (French) tribes almost immediately. These attacks continued, on and off, throughout the crossing. The Gauls' favourite tactic was to send huge boulders crashing down into the high, narrow passages the army was using, either to knock soldiers off the path or to block their way. At one particularly large blockade, Hannibal is said to have used an ancient mining trick. He lit a fire under the huge boulder and when the rock was as hot as possible, cold liquid (in this case vinegar) was thrown over it. The sudden change in temperature made the rock crack, making it easier to move out of the way.

The highest point of Hannibal's climb is reckoned to have been about 2,400 metres (8,000 feet) above sea level. The climb *up* the Alps from the French side was a relatively gentle slope. But going back *down* the Alps on the Italian side, was very, *very* steep. As well as the hostile locals, and then heavy falls of snow, Hannibal's army had to deal with a horribly dangerous descent, where falling to your death was a constant threat.

TROUBLEMAKERS

Once the fifteen-day trek across the Alps was over, Hannibal finally entered Italy with more than 25,000 soldiers, 6,000 horses and nearly all the thirty-seven elephants with which he'd set out. In the end, the Carthaginians never quite reached Rome, but Hannibal's forces did cause endless trouble for the Romans over the next three years. Whatever their fate, they'd undertaken one of the most daring and unusual journeys in history.

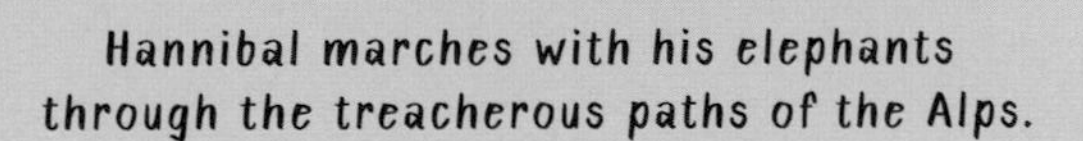

Hannibal marches with his elephants through the treacherous paths of the Alps.

IDA PFEIFFER

WRITER AND EXPLORER

Ida Laura Pfeiffer, from Austria, travelled alone and on a very tight budget, carrying with her only the bare essentials. She was headstrong and determined, one of several intrepid women travellers in history who challenged the standards of their day.

When Ida Pfeiffer was twelve years old, her home city of Vienna was captured by the French army. Unlike her mother, who thought it best to be polite and avoid trouble, little Ida showed her disgust at the invasion. At a triumphant parade of troops, she turned her back as the French emperor went past – this young girl snubbed Napoleon Bonaparte, one of the most powerful, ruthless and feared people in the world!

Pfeiffer always wanted to travel, but waited until both her sons had grown up and left home before she set off. Her writing about her adventures made her famous and funded further travels, although for most of her life her books were published anonymously. Her biggest hits were accounts of her journeys around the world.

1846–1848
SOUTH AMERICA, TAHITI, CHINA, INDIA, THE MIDDLE EAST, RUSSIA AND GREECE

Ida Pfeiffer was an eccentric mix of bold explorer and fussy nineteenth century European. She cheerfully put up with the slow pace and discomforts of travelling on the cheap, but she could also be rather sniffy about things she wasn't used to.

In Brazil, for example, she was less concerned with the beautiful landscape than the swarms of ants, mosquitoes and sand-fleas. She was happy to stay in the homes of local people, to study their culture and share their food, but she rarely liked any of them! She could be squeamish about values she didn't share.

1851–1854
ENGLAND, SOUTH AFRICA, MALAYSIA, BORNEO, INDONESIA, NORTH AMERICA, SOUTH AMERICA (AGAIN) AND AUSTRALIA

Pfeiffer completely ignored expert advice about the many dangers in the rainforests of Borneo and Indonesia, and went there anyway. She spent six months in the jungle and met tribes of headhunters known to be hostile to Europeans. She got on with them really well! However, she had to leave when it was clear that some of the tribe were getting ready to kill and eat her. She made a joke about being far too old and leathery to make a good dinner and then made her escape.

Pfeiffer was also a keen amateur scientist and collected thousands of specimens of plants, insects, sea life and minerals on her travels. It was on a trip to Madagascar, during which time she was briefly locked up by the fearsome Queen Ranavalona, that she caught a tropical disease, probably malaria. A year later, in 1858, she died from its effects after she had returned home to Vienna.

Ida Pfeiffer fends off mosquitoes in the wild.

GLOSSARY

AIR TRANSPORT AUXILIARY a British organisation which used non-military pilots to fly aircraft, supplies and troops around the UK during World War II.

AIR AND WATER PRESSURE the force with which air or water presses down on something (basically its weight). High up in the atmosphere there is less air, so air pressure is low; deep down in the oceans the huge weight of water above means pressure is high.

ARMADA the Spanish word for a fleet of navy ships.

ATMOSPHERE the layers of breathable gases which surround the Earth; our atmosphere is mostly made up of two gases: nitrogen and oxygen.

BLUEPRINTS technical drawings of buildings or machinery that are often printed on light-sensitive blue paper.

CIRCUMNAVIGATION a journey all the way around something; generally used to describe a journey around the whole world.

COLD WAR (1945–1991) a period of rivalry and suspicion between the USA and the USSR and the countries which supported them; each side tried to out-do the other in technology, weapons and political power.

COMPASS a device that tells you which direction you're going in; the most common type has a magnetised needle which always points to the Earth's magnetic north pole.

DESERT an area of land which is very dry and has very little rain or vegetation; deserts can be cold as well as hot.

DIPLOMAT someone hired by a government to act on behalf of that government in foreign countries or at international organisations; a country's official representative is most often called an 'ambassador'.

DRY GOODS an old-fashioned term to describe an everyday type of shop's stock, originally textiles and clothing but also including hardware and groceries.

EMBASSY a building in which ambassadors and other diplomats live or conduct their business.

EQUATOR the imaginary horizontal line running all the way around the middle of the Earth; at the equator, day and night are exactly the same length all year round.

GALLEON a large sailing ship with several decks, used mainly between the 1500s and 1700s; first built in Spain and later adopted by other European countries.

GLACIER a very large mass of densely packed ice; the majority of glacial ice is found in the polar regions, but also occurs in many mountainous areas around the world.

HYDROGEN the most common element in the universe; it is colourless, has no smell or taste and is extremely flammable.

ICE FLOE a large, flat, floating mass of sea ice; large areas of the Arctic are covered in ice floes.

MBE the Most Excellent Order of the British Empire; a medal originally awarded to non-combatants in World War I, but now given for public service or notable achievements.

NORTH AND SOUTH POLES the most northerly and most southerly points on the surface of the Earth, physically but not magnetically.

PHYSICS the scientific study of matter, energy and force, space and time; helps us examine and understand everything from the properties of a single atom to the structure of the entire universe.

POLYNESIA a region of the central and southern Pacific Ocean containing over one thousand islands, including Tonga, Samoa and Easter Island.

PRIVATEER a legalised pirate; a ship or individual who has official authorisation to attack vessels or places of a particular sort.

RAINFOREST a tropical forest which has high levels of rainfall all year round.

RAPIDS a section of a river where the water flows very fast, usually down a steep slope and often over shallower, more turbulent or rocky areas.

RENEWABLE ENERGY electricity made from things that don't run out, such as sunlight, wind, the movements of waves or tides, and heat from deep down under the ground.

ROMAN EMPIRE lands ruled in ancient times from the city of Rome in Italy; at its height, the Roman Empire covered most of Europe, a large part of the Middle East and the northern coastal strip of Africa.

SOVIET UNION (1922–1991) a group of east European states, principally Russia, ruled from the Russian capital city Moscow and characterised by its harsh, oppressive government.

STEAMBOAT a large boat, mainly used in the 1700s and 1800s, powered by steam which drove a propeller or a big paddle wheel; most were used on rivers and lakes, but some were ocean-going.

SUMMIT on a mountain, the very top, the highest point you can reach.

VALLEY OF THE KINGS a desert area close to the west bank of the River Nile in Egypt; it contains the underground tombs of over sixty Ancient Egyptian rulers and nobles, most famously King Tutankhamun.